THE
CALIFORNIA
FEELING

Half Dome, Yosemite

Text by PETER S. BEAGLE

Photographs by MICHAEL BRY

THE

CALIFORNIA

FEELING

With additional color photographs by

ANSEL ADAMS   J. R. EYERMAN

PHILIP HYDE   NEIL LAKATA

FRED LYON   JOHN WAGGAMAN

BARON WOLMAN

1969

DOUBLEDAY & COMPANY, INC.   GARDEN CITY, NEW YORK

Library of Congress Catalog Number 75-84395
Copyright © 1969 by Doubleday & Company, Inc.
All Rights Reserved
Printed In The United States of America
First Edition

For Enid
　　–Peter S. Beagle

For My Spiritual Uncle, Ted Castle
　　– Michael Bry

Table of Contents

Oak near Nicasio

1. The Feeling of California

(A PERSONAL VIEW)

A lot of the time, I don't even like the place. I don't like the politics, and I don't like the values behind the politics, and I don't like what's being done to the sky and the land and the water; and what I really don't like is that sense of having gotten here *almost* too late. My friend Jim Houston says that this is the California feeling, and that Juan Rodriguez Cabrillo, Joaquin Murietta, and John Muir undoubtedly suffered from it too. Jim was born and raised in San Francisco, and went to school in San Jose, and he grew up with that feeling, watching the orange groves being knocked over. But I came here from New York City, where you grow up knowing that there never was a golden time, that there was nothing to be too late for. You love New York now, or you don't love it at all. That's the New York feeling, anyway.

This book, hopefully, is about the California feeling. It is a book by a New Yorker who will never go back, but who remains a New Yorker in a curious, grumpy way that keeps him from taking the fact of being here too much for granted. We live within half an hour's drive of the beach (counting in stops for ice cream and new sand pails), and one January noon we went there for lunch with Jim and his wife, and Al Young, who is from Detroit. The sun was warm, and the sea was quiet, now and then stretching itself lazily. There were no other people on the beach. We ate cheese and salad, and drank wine; and Al sat on his heels in the sand, savoring everything, until at last he burst out laughing, and threw his arms wide and fell backward, saying, "Man, nobody does this!"

I think this book is a letter to New York. I can't imagine what else it could possibly be. It isn't a travel guide, and it isn't any sort of serious analysis of the state; and it certainly isn't that much-needed work on the way it really is to live in California. It's a grab-bag: a shapeless, disorderly rummage of scenes, impressions, memories, digressions, people, prejudices, days, places, misunderstandings, and mostly what I happened to be thinking about on that particular afternoon. As Thorne Smith said of his own books, you can probably start reading at any random page or section and "be equally mystified, if not revolted. I am myself." But if it were to be decoded and distilled, the message might run something like this:

"See, they don't have winter here. I mean, they have *a* winter — where I live, it's liable to rain any time between November and June, or all the time — but they don't have winter. The idea of it isn't carved into them right down to the chromosomes, the way it is with us. It makes a difference. I'm going to write a book about that difference one day, when I understand it better. It'll be called *The Social, Political, and Cultural Importance of Being Warm*.

"You have to have a car. I don't mean to get from one town to another, but just to get around — to go shopping, to visit friends, to go to a movie, to school, anywhere. California is flying slowly apart into things that aren't exactly towns, but more like the medieval feudal arrangements of houses ranged in the shadow of some local lord's thatched castle and paling of sharpened stakes. The lord, in this case, usually being a big shopping center. They don't have subways, of course; though there will eventually be one in the Bay Area, in spite of the people who are doing it. But one of the really serious problems in Watts, for instance, is that you can spend a couple of dollars and a couple of hours a day riding the buses to work in Los Angeles. The great urban areas move and feed like gigantic one-celled creatures, responding to needs and tropisms; but distances seem to be increasing. You know the way your body is disoriented by long jet flights from one time zone to another? There's a sense of that here all the time.

"They refill your coffee cup as often as you want in restaurants and diners; usually free, sometimes for a nickel. My wife says that's a Western thing, but I still associate it only with California. The coffee isn't nearly as good as New York coffee, but it's the spirit that counts, unless you really wanted coffee. Californians are friendlier than New Yorkers. Granted, so is the average Mexican bandit, but it's interesting to compare the two defense mechanisms. In New York, people go around like clenched fists, blind and furious, because they have to. Everything crowds in too closely — everything is screaming out there in the street. If you let your eyes focus on somebody, he'll come up to you and mug you, or proposition you, or breathe his hard luck, his death, all over you. Californians can still afford to smile and give a stranger directions. I don't think they give anything else any more freely than New Yorkers, but it sure looks like more. It's a matter of distance again.

"It's no easier to be poor out here than it is in the East — just warmer. One thing, though: garbage cans generally contain much more edible stuff than New York garbage cans. People throw things away earlier; supermarkets have big boxes of slightly stale vegetables sitting out in back, and they're usually grateful if you come around and pick over them. I also have it on excellent authority that the shoplifting scene is much better in California. I know several people who ate their way through four years of college for no more than the Army Surplus price of a very long overcoat.

"That's another thing. Going to school here is an altogether different experience than in New York. People who went to bile-colored elementary schools that had numbers instead of names, and then on to slaggy, small-windowed high schools and sidewalk universities like office buildings are just not like people who grew up going to schools that looked like schools. This has nothing to do with the quality of the education received, which is about the same. But in New York, being educated isn't supposed to be a sensual business. So we come out to California to do graduate work, and of course we go crazy.

"Native Californians do look different. When I first came to Stanford I suffered from snowblindness and vertigo for some time, until I began to get used to all those clean teeth and clean limbs; the sunny skin, the friendly, untroubled faces, the air of being the people that the movies and advertisements were made for and about, and of knowing it. I used to suspect that they exposed all the ugly babies on hillsides. It was almost a relief to wander into Berkeley in the spring and discover the sallow, wary, messed-up New York faces there. Incidentally, one reason that the hippie world is much less attractive in the East Village than in the Haight-Ashbury is that the New York faces don't look right with flowers in their hair. The faces know it, too, and it obviously cramps everything.

"The country and the city are still mixed up together in California. Back home — I do say that sometimes — the country was where you went in the summer, either to a camp or to a rented cottage, and you knew when you were in the country because of the green, and the cows. But here, although they're certainly working on it, the edges aren't that distinct yet; the idea of greenness hasn't yet become *foreign*, as it is in New York. You can still find pieces of wild country within earshot of the freeways — not doing anything use-ful, or even especially beautiful: just being wild. (Here in Santa Cruz, the deer come almost into town, and once in a while you see coyotes on the U. C. campus.) Doom broods over wild California: it will be paved from end to end, and parking spaces painted all over it. (Magnificently ironic, that Governor Ronald Reagan should have suggested for Vietnam what is so much more likely to happen to California.) This is a part of the California feeling — this certainty of irreparable loss — and somehow the tension sharpens your awareness of what remains. *While you can, while you can. Don't just look at it, learn it, while you can.*

"When you come out here, remember that California is a stage, a setting, in a way that no other part of the country is. You come to play California as an entertainer would play the old Palace — repertoire ready, routines rehearsed, lighting all planned, arrangements arranged — and if you don't go over, whatever your act may be, you really will feel as though you were being sent back to four-piece pit bands, night buses, and cold, small dressing rooms with one bulb and one mirror. I'm not sure what it is in California that puts us all onstage, doing our things, but I know it's real. It informs almost everything that happens here, conscious or unconscious, public or personal. A lot of good New York routines die in California: the trick is to stay loose, to find your act and your audience at the same time, while you're on. The houses are curious and adventurous — more so than in New York — but they get bored easily.

"I've lived here for six years now. My brother and his wife came to stay this year, and they wandered around saying the sort of things that our grandparents must have said in New York nearly sixty years ago. *This is it, we really are here. I can't believe it. I just can't believe it. We live here.* In this country, people only talk that way about California and New York, and neither place deserves it. No place really deserves that kind of wonder.

"But I have it too, even now, knowing better. It probably has a lot to do with the fact

California coast near Sonoma

that I grew up in California, in the real sense—married, had children, did what I could, as the song says. But I still feel what I felt that first day at the San Francisco Airport: twenty-one, sleepy, blinking in the white morning. In the late afternoon, sometimes, I walk down and up a narrow path to the meadow, to bring the horses home. The dog and my son run on ahead, and three or four cats usually follow, complaining and getting lost in the weeds. Standing on a thin rise of ground, I can see our house from the meadow, in the slow, dusty light through the fir trees and the redwoods; and if I stand on tiptoe I can practically catch the brimming tin brilliance at the edge of everything that is almost always the ocean. *I'm here. I can't believe it.*

"I didn't say *love*, New York. You can't love California, they'll kill you. But I wonder at it still. I wonder at it. Anyway, this was just to let you know where I am now. Good-by, New York."

Much of this book is based on a series of voyages up and down California that Michael Bry and I made during the course of a year. Mike is German and Chilean and American— not in neat geological strata, but all together, the way children roll different colors of clay into each other. He is an artist, a solid harmonica player (with a natural country sound), and one of the world's great improvisational cooks, given a couple of cans and a few onions. Mike is also very comfortable to be quiet with, late in the day, with fifty miles still to go, everything discussed, and the five-thirty gloomies coming on. He comes into this book much more often than he is mentioned.

We did our traveling in a 1957 Volkswagen bus named Renata Tebaldi. She went everywhere, *andante* and in 4/4 time, but she got where she was going, and she put up graciously with the erratic tenors. Mike built a bed in the back, which turned out to be so comfortable, and made Renata herself so self-sufficient, that he said with a sigh, "It's sure too bad both of us are a fella." She smelled of dust and cheese and unwashed sleeping bags, and at night she made small creaking, pinging noises as everybody settled down.

2. It Isn't Berkeley yet . . .

(SANTA CRUZ AREA)

I'll start with Santa Cruz, because I live here. It's a good place to begin. Most of the elements that meet in the dream of California can be found in Santa Cruz. It's a coast town with a good, soft climate most of the year, and it's been the most popular seaside resort north of Santa Barbara since the nineteenth century. People retire to Santa Cruz, to fish and be warm, and to grow flowers. You can tell a good deal about this town just by the gardens. Only people with a lot of time, and not too many other things to love, could have lawns and hedges and gardens like these.

Seen from the hills near the university campus, Monterey Bay seems perfectly level with the town; even tipped up slightly, so that one more sail out there will surely start the sea sliding over the edge, spilling quietly down over the white and red houses. It has never happened like that, but the cliffs are soft and shaly, and every winter the waves scoop away more of them. That's why the beaches are so good. The road along the cliffs broke in two a few years back.

Like Monterey, forty miles down the coast, Santa Cruz began as a mission site and went through a period of extensive cattle ranching in the Mexican days. But it was never important politically or militarily; it didn't really exist as a city until 1850 or thereabouts, when eastern merchants started building shops and homes around the old mission plaza. There's plenty of adobe and red tile, but most of the oldest houses here are of wood: small, sharp New England houses, still holding themselves tightly braced for the New England winter. In a certain sense, Mexican California ends at Santa Cruz, as the redwoods begin.

The town has grown very slowly, even with the doubled postwar population, which stands at about 30,000 today. Heavy industry has never located here, and probably never will. There are canneries and a chewing-gum factory; lumber yards, frozen-food plants, and an old-established tannery. But the new presence of the University of California is changing Santa Cruz swiftly now. The downtown area is growing steadily out and up: small storefront blocks are being replaced by high-rise apartments, and Santa Cruz is actually developing a skyline. The total effect is awkward and characterless, like a sudden bosom on a girl who was designed to be willowy. It'll probably look more natural in five or ten years.

The architectural glory of the town are the many Victorian houses still standing. I'm cranky and perverse enough in my tastes to be pretty sure that I'd have detested them if

Surfers of Santa Cruz

Beach at Santa Cruz

I'd been around when they were going up. All alike, all in a row like that. They're really incredibly silly and vulgar, most of them: like great cupcakes, with their spires and cupolas and bay windows; their turrets that bubble up everywhere, as though the cook forgot to prick the crust; their gingerbread scrollwork. My images are all of pastry, because that's the way they are. Cyrano's buddy Ragueneau, the poetry-writing baker, might have designed them all. Oh, they're awful. Low camp.

I love them. They're disappearing now, one by one, and the places where they grew have been sown with gas stations. My time in California has made me wonder very seriously if I am one of those people who are doomed to love only the doomed things, automatically. I hope not; it's boring and dangerous. But these old houses, for all their rich pastry weight, have a human gaiety that isn't being replaced. Like that gray monster on the hill overlooking Front and Laurel. Victorian or no, there's never been an era in which that thing would have been accepted as a normal, proper place to live. But when you know it, it's as light as a bunch of balloons; soap bubbles clinging together. I know the cosmos doesn't give a damn—nor should it—but I don't think a gas station is a fair exchange for that one.

The beach is still Santa Cruz's main industry. On any warm weekend, nearly a quarter of a million people may be spread along the county coast and picnicking in the redwood parks; and Santa Cruz has no competition for fifty miles in either direction. In the summer, beach property rents like front seats at the Last Judgment, and the area between the wharf and the boardwalk is a maelstrom until late at night. The traffic is too heavy for the old beach streets to contain. There was an attempt made recently to turn Schwan Lake (a graceful, quiet pond where wild ducks live) into a parking lot for the beach just across the lake. It failed, because people get aroused and organized about things like that, but the city will try again. They have no choice.

The surfers come here all year round. I've seen scores at a time riding their boards off Pleasure Point with a cold, stinging rain coming down. Golfers are the only other people I know who do that sort of thing. Santa Cruz has always been considered the best surfing north of Malibu, but the real boom only began in this decade. Today there are three places in town that specialize in custom-made surfboards, pouring them out of foam plastic and coating them with fiberglass and resin. The national Pro-Am championship competition is held here, at Steamer Lane.

When the surf is running, it's almost impossible to drive along the cliff roads for the panel trucks and station wagons, and the salt-blond, orange-tanned kids in their rubber wet suits. There are usually a few psychedelic cars in the crowd, and the Iron Cross and the peace symbol seem interchangeable, up to a point. But hippies don't surf, and real surfers—the ones out there in the rain—aren't very hip. The ones I've met have been generally friendly, open, and—at this point in their lives—involved with nothing but the water. It's mystic and middle-class at once; Babbitt and Ishmael in the same skin. Maybe that's what attracts the hippies.

It's a lovely thing. I can't think of any other sport I'd rather be good at, except possibly sailing and gliding. I've never ridden a surfboard, but I know the basics of bodysurfing, and every now and then I pick up a wave the way you're supposed to, remembering to press my arms flat at my sides, and to keep my head and shoulders tucked down in the water. For a few seconds, it's all there—the limitless, unimaginable power lifting me and hurling me in, faster than I've ever felt myself going; the howling all around me, and me breathless, terrified, and yet quiet, enchantedly unharmed, tapped into the power, if I don't move, if I don't lose it, going with it as long as I can. It's like sex, of course. There's no question about that.

The boardwalk—there's a world; there's a strange, sunny jungle. To understand it, you have to understand something of what it is like to be young in a town like Santa Cruz. One fourth of the population here is over sixty-five years old, and despite the changes of the last few years, Santa Cruz is still geared to that fact economically and socially. For that other quarter of the population which is under twenty-one, there is nothing to do after eight or nine P.M., and not much before then.

Downtown on a Friday or Saturday night, Pacific Street is full of cars, but they aren't going anywhere. The sidewalks are bright and silent. Everything's closed. After a while, you start spotting the same cars as they make the circuit: down to the beach and back up Ocean Street, and around again. Roll along in second, call out the window at girls, try to decide whether it's worth driving over the mountains to San Jose or Santa Clara. I used to do that in Pittsburgh with Reggie, so many warm, wasted Saturday nights when I was seventeen. We wound up in Kinsman, Ohio, like that one night.

The boardwalk. I used to know two girls, twin sisters, who spent most of their time down there. Whenever they cut school, or ran away from home — which was often — they were pathetically easy to find. I don't think they liked the boardwalk all that well, but their friends were there; and it was only on the boardwalk that they had any idea of who they were, or where they were. Both of them were very pretty and intelligent. They were fifteen years old then.

I never walk around there without thinking of them, without trying to see the way it was for them. Some afternoons there'll be hundreds of kids swirling in front of the Cocoanut Grove: peacoats, paisley shirts, and bell-bottom pants color the air like autumn. They're high school age, mostly, but I see girls of twelve and thirteen quite often. The boys are hardly ever that young. Boots and blazoned denim jackets move among them, in another dimension — the motorcycle gangs come down from San Jose. On weekends there are dances at the Grove, and the police are present in layers, in coats.

The kiddie underworld, Al Young calls it. Nothing ever seems to be happening — they're just wandering with their little radios, waiting for something to happen. But it's all going on just at the edge of understanding, as it goes on in your animal world and mine: the small maimings and matings, deaths and devourings. Judy and Dana used to meet their friends here, and the boys. They smoked pot, and they fooled with LSD; and sometimes they let themselves find themselves under the boardwalk with the boys, headachy and uncomfortable, high but not high enough, looking out at the water.

Santa Cruz is going through a child scare right now. Nominally it's drugs: marijuana is turning up in the glove compartments of all the family Mustangs; and babyfaced narcotics agents are assigned to bust pot-and-acid rings at the high school. Films and lectures about LSD are very hot tickets. The *Sentinel* runs a series of articles explaining how you can tell if your son or daughter is turning on. Adults who can't stand rock music are becoming experts on such euphemistic lyrics as "Strawberry Fields Forever" and "Rainy Day Women #12 and 35." Santa Cruz has been designated one of the bigger drug drops in Northern California, and an express stop on the runaways' underground railway as well. Various groups of concerned parents blame everything on Earl Warren.

But I don't know. The fear is real, but I think sometimes that it's as much a fear of the children as it is a fear for them. That newspaper series was almost like the instructions they put out for the home front during wartime. How to recognize enemy planes; how to detect spies and saboteurs. How to decode your kid's lapel buttons. The Santa Cruz police have been harassing even straight-looking teen-agers lately; and if there's one matter on which cops are generally experts, it's the things their towns are afraid of at any given moment.

Sunbathers at Santa Cruz

Is this a California thing, to go into this book? I don't know. I live here, in the hills north of Santa Cruz, and I don't even catch a lot of what's going on in town. But the drug scene is still biggest in this state, and California is still the region most conscious of its adolescents as a subculture, to be adored and rousted, explained and exploited, studied and ignored. I'm pretty sure there's a direct connection.

Judy and Dana weren't enemy planes, or the advance guard of a new civilization. They were nice girls, vaguely kind, and curiously, sadly innocent; bored and lonely all the way through. The worst that could ever be said about them is that they had no resources inside themselves. The muscles had never been developed. There are a hell of a lot of people like them.

Santa Cruz is changing, all the same. When we moved here in 1963, I was the only beard in town, or near enough, and people stared at me when I went shopping. Now I'm a reasonably respectable citizen — a little scruffy, perhaps, but utterly straight by contrast with what's checking out ahead of me in Safeway. I'm getting to feel like part of the power elite.

It's a sudden and drastic business, of course, this transition from a wealthy, sedate beach town to an academic community; one in which the university will be an incalculably dominating force. UCSC plans to expand slowly, but inevitably there will be nearly 30,000 students on campus — the population of the entire town today. Santa Cruz is much more likely to become Santa Barbara than Berkeley, but many people are angrily and unhappily waiting for trouble with the kids. The town's few Negroes are growing perceptibly more

Seal Rock near Santa Cruz

visible, and the police are attending riot seminars and asking for money to buy some of those fancy new anti-mob weapons. What you fear most is usually what happens.

There was a place called the Hip Pocket Bookstore in Santa Cruz for a couple of years. It was a good store, or it would have been, but the young owners spent most of their time *en épatant le bourgeoisie*. They *épated* them something fierce, one way and another, between politics and pornography; but essentially by turning the bookstore into a gypsy-seedy den full of uniquely aggressive-looking hippies. Oh, it was a wicked place, ironically contiguous to a hotel lobby where old men and women sat all day watching TV. I never knew who had the pot and LSD concession at the Hip Pocket, but that was where you went.

The John Birchers and the fundamentalists reacted quite properly. They held meetings, preached savage sermons, wrote letters to the newspaper, and sent their children into the bookstore to buy copies of *Candy*. The shooting really started when they goaded the police to close down a Hip Pocket exhibition of Walter Chappell photographs, several of which featured male genitalia. The police, foreseeing the outcome, tried to avoid action, but an organized telephoning campaign tied up their switchboard so thoroughly that they were actually forced to move. They confiscated the exhibit, and charged the Hip Pocket's owners with showing obscene photographs. The American Civil Liberties Union took the case, and got it thrown out of court.

It went on like that for quite a while. The Hip Pocket happily filled the role of town menace to perfection, and the Birchers were remarkably obnoxious for a minor-league operation. The thing only ended when the bookstore went bankrupt: not notably due to the right-wingers' boycott, but because very few of its liberal allies bought books there. The Hip Pocket's right to exist was a matter of uncompromisable principle, but the sullen stares of the hippies put off even the best-willed civil libertarians. Raids and fulminations boosted sales occasionally, but not enough. You can't run many businesses on hooha.

Today there's another bookstore where the Hip Pocket used to be: a quiet place, with no name. It is run by a co-op, which has also set up a coffee shop called The Catalyst in the hotel, and intends in time to take the whole place over. There are movies, concerts, readings, and — rarest and most important — a nice place to sit down without buying anything. The grumpy hippies are mostly gone (where to, I wonder?), but the new bookstore sells everything that the Hip Pocket sold, except pot. It appears to be doing excellent business with all political, religious, and emotional camps.

Over in Ben Lomond, the great hippie crisis has settled down to a wary truce. The merry merchants still discourage the young people's patronage, but they don't throw Molotov cocktails into their psychedelic bus anymore, and that must certainly be counted as a gain. It's a very odd story. I know something about it because the group of hippies who took over the abandoned resort lodge in Ben Lomond were talking with my next-door neighbor for a while about renting some of his land. And I know the young lawyer who got onto the case after the bombing incident. He wasn't hired; he just went up there. His name is Bob Ludlow.

Ben Lomond is one of several small towns in the shaggy, wet redwood country immediately northeast of Santa Cruz. There's some lumbering going on in the area, and a little mining, but all the towns live mainly off the summer people. A number of hippies had been living around Ben Lomond for some time, and when a place called Holiday Lodge went out of business, they made a deal with the landlord and moved in. That was early in 1967.

The Ben Lomond people went mad. It had all the old elements of the first day of school in New Orleans or Birmingham. Several of the hippies were local kids, and that may even have made things worse. The NO HIPPIES signs went up in stores and restaurants, and there was serious public talk about forming vigilante groups. One of the boys was beaten up on the main street by a gang of grown men. Two people happened to be asleep in the bus when the fire bomb was tossed through the door. They weren't hurt.

As I say, it's all gotten considerably quieter since then. Bob Ludlow (who is from Ben Lomond himself; he went to school with a couple of the Holiday Lodge hippies) moved around among the citizenry, reminding them that discrimination, assault, and conspiracy are regarded as criminal acts even when committed against people with long hair. This appeared to startle everybody quite a lot, almost as much as the fact that the hippies had actually asked a lawyer for help. "Who'd have thought they had enough sense?" is the way it was most commonly put.

When I went with Mike to visit Holiday Lodge, I didn't think I'd like it. I'm not much for group living, which is probably my deepest objection to the hippie way. The drugs scare me; and I think that the ethic of love is as much a surface matter with many hippies as it is with their church-going parents. I remember something that happened when we were in the Panhandle, watching the Diggers feed everybody. It was a funny, silly, pretty scene: these good-looking, city-looking young people dancing barefoot on the winter grass like strolling players, while somebody's phonograph played Bach until the big dog got excited and bumped into it. Nobody looked all that undernourished, but what the hell. I've known hippie kids who were living on chocolate milk.

One of the Diggers was a thin blond boy with that kind of glassy skin that never grows hair and never tans. He looked about seventeen, and he was hugging himself with ineffable delight as he watched the hot stew being served out and everyone falling to. We talked for a while, about his family in Menlo Park, about the chances of his going back to school (he thought he might like to teach some day); but mostly about the Diggers, who really have been one of the gifts to come out of the hippie adventure. They give things away, which is genuine subversion, and that stuff is harder to come by than Senator Eastland imagines.

"The beautiful part of it is that we don't have a leader. They can't understand that. The newspapers write about somebody and they say he's the one, and then the fuzz come

Hippie Ranch near Ben Lomond

around and bust him. So somebody else comes forward, whoever's needed. Everybody's a leader, whenever he's needed."

The Diggers beg and con and cadge their dry goods, and every so often they come into money. In the fine old American tradition, there is a whopping amount of money being made off hippies — much of it by other hippies. Some of the Diggers' friends are in a position to get a little of their own back.

"You take Bill Graham." Graham is a very sharp promoter who puts on the dances at the Fillmore Auditorium. "Bill Graham gives us money pretty regularly now," the boy said. "The Airplane and the Grateful Dead put the squeeze on him. They said if he didn't do it, they'd never work for him again." He laughed, eager and happy and unmalicious.

"See, Bill Graham's a real nice guy, but he's Jewish, and you know — " I still think that Mike and I kept our faces quiet, but he caught something. I felt sorry for him then, because he was embarrassed, and because I really liked him. He went on, "Well, he's a European, and I guess he has this old-country thing about bread. You can understand it."

Anyway, Holiday Lodge turned out nice. The setting was lovely, for one thing: rich, tangled land just off U.S. 9, a lot like the country where I live. Redwoods and creeping myrtle and poison oak; a stream at the bottom of the hill, and blackberries. Hippie works best outdoors, I think. The Haight-Ashbury has always been a bad, drizzly place, but in Golden Gate Park any way of living seems natural and sensible. In the city, as the man says in *La Vida*, you get swallowed by a horse.

It was a lazy morning when we were there. There had been a big party the night before, and people were moving slowly. The place felt like a summer camp, with the cabins and the barefoot, shirtless boys; and even one big cabin like a combined office and social hall, with overstuffed chairs and couches, a soft-drink cooler, job schedules tacked up on the walls, and camper art posted for Parents' Weekend. I'm not making fun of the feeling — it was familiar and comfortable.

We met Zack in the big cabin. Zack is as much the head counselor as there is such a thing around Holiday Lodge. The insistence that they have no leader is common to most hippie tribes, but Zack hardly bothers with the usual disclaimer. "Somebody has to keep things going. Not run them, just — well, like stuff has to be picked up." He has a long face, dominated by a big, sensitive mouth. Thin hair that waves laterally. Very earnest hands, with flat fingers.

This picking-things-up business makes Holiday Lodge fairly rare among the hippie colonies that I've run across or know about. Zack kept coming back to it. "We don't have a rules hangup, it's not like that. But when people live together there's just things everybody has to do. I think everything you do should be a turn-on. I think cleaning up your room can be as satisfying an experience as sex. It's all part of the same thing."

He pointed to one of the scribbled-over lists on the wall. "There aren't like regular jobs, but that's some of the stuff that always needs to be done. Cut wood, work around the garden, clean up in the kitchen, collect garbage. Whatever you see. If you see a broken window, you fix it; or if you're doing something else, you write down there's a broken window. It'll get fixed. If you find a cat mess, you clean it up — if there's a short circuit, or a drain backing up, a bulb burned out. You do whatever you see has to be done."

Another boy came in, pink-faced and smiling, with a pointed golden beard. They both said, "Hey, man!" and their voices were full of shy delight. The newcomer went over to Zack and hugged him. It was short and stumbling, probably because of us, but it was real. Zack said, "Hey — how are you?"

Holiday Lodge rents for five hundred dollars a month. Everyone who lives there — about thirty people that day — pays twenty-five dollars a month into a central kitty, which is another interesting difference between the Lodge and most other communes. The money is, for all practical purposes, handled by Zack and a few other members of the group that first moved into the camp. Zack sounds almost like Barry Goldwater, talking about it. "We figure anybody who wants to can make twenty-five a month. There's all kinds of work around here, in Santa Cruz, Felton, Boulder Creek. If somebody really can't scrounge up the bread, that's one thing — but we've had a couple of guys come through thinking this was like, you know, a free ride. It isn't. We're serious about this."

It seems to be working all right; at least during the summer, with jobs like dishwashing, waiting tables, lawnmowing and babysitting easy to come by. Nobody feels violated by having to make twenty-five dollars. "It's like the song," Marcus said. Marcus is a Negro, the only one in the camp, tall and easy. "*Sing for your supper and you'll get breakfast — song-birds always eat.* That's what we're doing, singing for our suppers." What kind of a hippie quotes Rodgers and Hart, for God's sake?

We wandered from cabin to cabin, talking to people, stroking cats, listening to guitars. The cabins themselves are beautifully made: high and solid, with plenty of windows and huge double doors, often on both sides of the house. Each cabin is heated by a big wood stove. Some motel. It's a hell of a deal for twenty-five a month.

Curious feeling the place has — hardly modern hippie at all, but more like the little camouflaged pockets of Bohemia that used to turn up in the strangest places six or seven years ago. That was California to me too — pot, and mattresses on the floor, and those huge balloon lampshades from Cost-Plus. Bead curtains and Madras bedspreads; worn cartons full of books and records. Even the guitar-playing around here is the three-finger style that was so big in the early 1960s. I don't know what the exact difference is between those times and these. Amplification, I guess.

Nobody's married, but things look much more domestic than sinful. The girls were cooking or unpacking or moving stuff around (I hadn't thought of it till Mike pointed it out, but it's true: hippie/beat/Bohemian girls tend to be earth-mother types; buxom, sturdy *kibbutzniks*, making the desert bloom), while the boys made bookshelves, or sat in the sun with guitars and beer. In Dave and Jenny's cabin, she was cleaning the ashes out of the stove while he sat on the bed grating lily bulbs into a bowl. You make little balls out of the shreds, roll them in dough, and fry them.

Dave and Jenny have been living together for several years. They came here from San Francisco a month ago. Before San Francisco they lived around Denver for a while, and before that it was Mexico, Seattle, Santa Fe, Mill Valley. This is familiar too, the western wandering. People are always coming and going, suddenly splitting for Big Sur down the dark, whispery coast road. Orbits cross your own: you rise and set in one another's skies, and vanish into the crowded night, until your co-ordinates bring you near again — in a week, in a couple of months, in a few years. Time is different in California.

Where to after Holiday Lodge? Dave's thinking about Mexico again, maybe in the winter. Jenny is very high on British Columbia, though she's never been there. That seems to be the place right now; funny how fast the new dream gets around. "They're begging people to come out to British Columbia and homestead," Jenny says. "It's like the old land rush days."

Would you like that, homesteading? "It'd be a change. I'd like to go take a look, anyway." She's a pretty girl. I didn't notice it right away.

The only thing that's really hippie about Holiday Lodge is the overlay of mysticism. Zack talked about the regular meetings where everyone sits silently in a circle, holding hands, and about the itinerant gurus they invite to talk to them. Someone has made a shrine in a little cedar grove: there is a kind of altar, a statue, the fat stumps of candles. The holders are twisted strips of copper, nailed to the trees.

I don't know when it came back this time. Maybe with Ginsberg, maybe with Leary. I'm willing to agree that a few hundred choruses of Hare Krishna are an improvement over one round of "Stand up, stand up for Jesus," but not that much of an improvement. It's a strange time. The God of Cecil B. DeMille and George Wallace is dead, and people are studying the *I Ching* and the Tarot. In a ghost town named Casper, up near Mendocino, there's a colony of young people taking lessons in the Cabala. Astrology is big again. Books on Edgar Cayce and other seers are selling like crazy. The Maharishi is planning to tour college campuses with the Beach Boys. There is a deep wish in the air just now for some better reality, however inflexible it may turn out to be.

Oh, we met Peanuts. Peanuts was lying on her bed, wearing a housecoat patterned like a Persian rug; not doing anything, just lying there with her hands folded and her ankles crossed. A guitar lay on the bed next to her, and there were two packs of cigarettes on the guitar. Sweet, sleepy, secret-voiced Peanuts. Peanuts is the girl that you dream of meeting when you dream of letting go. When you hear somebody railing hysterically about those filthy, degenerate, loose-living hippies, he's really talking about the way Peanuts looks. He always has been.

I don't know anything else about her — where she was from, how old she was (seventeen, eighteen, no more), whom she was living with; what she liked to do when she wasn't lying in the noon darkness of the cabin. She said, "I go all the way back. Some of us have been together for three years. I'm like one of the originals."

She was a little concerned about the rainy season. This redwood country turns into a cold marsh once the rain starts. The sun doesn't get down through the trees, and places just stay wet between November and June. There won't be many people staying on when the rain comes, Peanuts thinks. Even a few of the originals may try to make it to Mexico.

What will you do, Peanuts, in the cold? "Oh, I'll stay." She smiles very slowly, not at us. "I just have a feeling I'm needed here. I'll stay here."

It's raining as I write this, flashing silver in my dark window, hissing like fire. The ground is swollen with rain, creaking with it. Two years ago, it kept up like this for twenty-one days. The dog has come inside, although he's afraid of all the cats. Over the hill, the bulldozer was roaring desolately all afternoon. I think it's gotten stuck in the mud. It does that every winter, like hibernating.

Marcus, the Negro, said something that morning when I asked what he thought would become of the Holiday Lodge community. "Oh, it'll break up. It's supposed to." I didn't get it, and Marcus smiled. I still wonder about Marcus and that Rodgers and Hart song.

"We'll all take it away with us," he said. "When we've got it working right, when we *know* it, then we can all walk away free, by ourselves, and live like this wherever we are. This place doesn't matter. What happens to us, that's what matters."

Kings Canyon

The Shape of the Land

Juniper root

BARON WOLMAN. *Marina, Los Angeles*

J. R. EYERMAN. *Los Angeles*

NEIL LAKATA. *Downtown Los Angeles*

NEIL LAKATA. *Golden State and Pasadena Freeway Interchange*

ANSEL ADAMS. *Livermore Valley*

FRED LYON. *Sea Ranch, Northernmost Sonoma Coast*

MICHAEL BRY. *Panamint Mountains*

ANSEL ADAMS. *Lone Pine Peak, Sierra Nevada*

ANSEL ADAMS. *Joshua Tree National Monument*

Banner Peak

Mendocino coast

I know a man named Max who lives way the hell back in the Big Sur in an old stone house. He has lived here for a long time; not as long as Jeffers, but near it. Max was here when Henry Miller was still sweating it out in Brooklyn.

Big Sur is very nearly a closed community these days. Land prices are prohibitive, and the few available houses are passed along a private waiting list, like apartments in Paris. "They're so damn worried about keeping business out," Max says, "they've fixed it so nobody but a millionaire can afford to move in. Millionaires are lousy company. The Sur's going to hell."

People come and go around Max's house all during the warm weather. High school kids, university couples from Berkeley and San Francisco, musicians, potters — classifiable people — and the wanderers: young and old, male and female, black and white, open and shut, and everything in between. They sleep at Max's house, chip in for food—or don't—read the books that lie all over his bedroom floor, ride horses, make music, sit in the sun, mess around with old cars and pumps and washing machines. Max moves among them, friendly and casual, but guarded too, in his shaggy, muttering way. Tomorrow they will be gone, or next week, and in the rainy winter Max will be alone.

Point Lobos

Elk Head

Marin County Buckeyes

Sierra Sunset

Bay Trees in Coast Range

I like Death Valley; in the winter, anyway. One of the ironies of the 1849 emigrants'
suffering journey across the Valley is that they were paying their visit at the height of the tourist
season: in December, when the temperatures are generally comfortable, and there's plenty of
water, vegetation, and animal life around, if you know where to look. The Indians who observed
the Jayhawkers and the Manly-Bennett party from the slopes of the Panamint Mountains
had been living in Death Valley for a thousand years. It's hard to blame them for not
showing the desperate white men where to look. Squanto was a nut who did the Massachusetts
Indians no favor, teaching the Pilgrims to plant corn.

Anyway, the valley is a startlingly beautiful place, especially for one brought up
on legends of its broiling barrenness. The most celebrated attraction is color, from the rich,
coarse warpaint of the craters and the mountains, to the white salt flats, the green mesquite
and creosote bush and the smoky purple sagebrush; to the more delicate oxidized greens, roses,
and ochres of Artists' Drive. But the range of textures is the more lasting memory
—the great rock masses, smashed and scrambled by volcanic action; the alluvial fans
and fossilized lakes; the raking salt pinnacles of the Devil's Golf Course; the bril-
liant, flood-burnished pebbles in Mosaic Canyon; the soft rhythm of the dunes. Tolkien's
dwarfs would like this country. They'd say it had good bones. The silence of Death
Valley is a texture too, and ought to be mentioned on the tourist maps, as surely as Dante's
View and Zabriski Point. When I think of the valley, the first thing I remember
is a morning when, wandering around the ruins of the Harmony Borax Works, we looked
up to see a military jet coming over, flying very low. It slid over us in absolute
silence, and was away down the valley before the mutter of its passage reached us. Three others
followed, one at a time: each low and floating, making no sound. We might have been
far under the ocean, watching slow, lean shadows crossing above our belled heads.

Bolinas Lagoon

Mount San Jacinto

Mendocino Coast

Marin County Barn

Cattle and Mountains

*Joshua Tree National Monument. They aren't trees, but gigantic lilies, which may
grow 50 feet high and live 400 years. The Mormons of San Bernardino gave them the name
because of their upstretched, sunstopping arms, and it becomes them. They have an Old
Testament outsize vitality — they might as easily be cursing or challenging God as calling on
him. In the spring, when the rest of the Mojave blooms for a moment, red and white
and gold (there are even lupines and poppies some years, for a moment), the Joshua trees
put forth huge, toothy flowers: green, graceless, and tender, like some big girls.*

*This is the southern edge of the High Desert; both Palm Springs and the Salton Sea
are visible from Salton View. The presence of the Mojave dominates Southern California in the
same way that the knowledge of the Sierra Nevada and the Cascades does the North. It
isn't as aggressively, immediately, magnificent (you can't not love the Sierra — you're not given
the option); its strength is slow and secret. Yet it occurs to me that I know far more
desert nuts than I know true mountain people. Most of the people who spend a lot of time
in the Sierra go there for one or several specific reasons. They ski, they climb, they*

hike; they hunt and fish, or they take horses and go off on pack trails. They're in the mountains to do something, and they can tell you what it is.

But the desert people seem to go out just to be in the desert. I never see them doing anything, though there are proper recreational things to do: hunt rocks, pick flowers, study the birds and animals, explore caves, buy real estate. (Between the military, the highway towns, and the growing number of retirees and winter residents, there are now about 200,000 people living in the High Desert.) I meet them standing around their campers, parked off the pale roads among the yuccas and the cholla cactus, not doing anything, just being in the desert. They've been coming out every winter or spring for years, some of them; ten, fifteen years, since the war. They stay in towns named Twentynine Palms, Joshua Tree, Morongo Valley. (Despite the valiant efforts of the men who build and sell communities these days, that old American gift of names is not quite dead.)

By and large, the desert people say the same things, especially the ones who come up from Los Angeles or San Diego. "It's so quiet here. And the air is so good."

There's an interesting contrast between Mount Shasta and Mount Lassen. Lassen is a blunt, beat-up, homely mountain, but it becomes dignified and almost handsome as you draw close to it. Shasta, on the other hand, is unbelievably beautiful until you're about twenty miles away. Between one mile and another, it suddenly collapses into ordinariness; a small mountain, not unattractive, but without the least suggestion of the translucent delicacy that dominated the horizon all day yesterday. You never see it happen.

3. Where's Your Soul?

(MONTEREY-CARMEL AREA)

To get to Monterey, you go south through short-handled hoe country: Watsonville, Castroville ("The Artichoke Capital of the World") — miles of lettuce, strawberry, tomato, and artichoke fields, with Mexican-Americans working in them for very little. Moss Landing is on the way, too — a tiny harbor village that has been a whaling station and a sardine packer, and still maintains a fishing fleet; but now belongs pretty much to Kaiser and the PG&E. The two great plants loom and glow through the fog at night like the steamboat that ran down Huck and Jim's raft.

I like Monterey, though I don't know it well. I've been there often, but almost always as part of a high-pressure stream of cars being squeezed through the narrow streets and squirted from landmark to landmark; from the Old Custom House to the house where Robert Louis Stevenson spent three months in 1879. But unlike most of the historic places that fifth-grade classes get *schlepped* to, Monterey feels as though real people have lived here. All those balconied wood-and-adobe houses had voices in them once, and doors opening and closing; footsteps, and the sounds of silverware.

Monterey has been a living, functioning city as long as there has been a place called Alta California. It was the capital of the Spanish and Mexican state from 1770 until the United States seized it in 1846; and the outlines of the old presidio town, and the several other towns that Monterey has been, are still quite clear. There was never much important industry or agriculture, but it was always full of somebody's soldiers; and the tourists came in with the Southern Pacific in 1878. And there were the canneries, of course, for more than thirty years, when Monterey was "The Sardine Capital of the World."

But the sardines stopped running after World War II, and Cannery Row is a ghost street now, with the old buildings looking as gray and frail and ragged as the stuff that tent caterpillars leave on trees. Tourism and the military are the main industries again. The Army is in the Presidio, Fort Ord is a few miles away; and the motels, gas stations, used-car lots, Tas-T-Freezes and Doggie Diners are pouring along U.S. 1. Conditions change and change, but Monterey is still alive, and it still has secrets.

I wonder, by the way, why no one has tried to reclaim the canneries and set them up as artists' studios. When nothing more can be gotten out of a place, it's time for the artists and poets to move in. The Row might see one more spring, different from the others.

The Monterey Jazz Festival, which has been held here since 1958, is considered to be the

Monterey Adobe

best in the country, both in terms of the music itself and of the atmosphere in which it gets played. As always in California, the setting has a lot to do with it. The Monterey Fairgrounds, where the Festival is staged, has a medieval air about it that suggests racing on the green, shooting at the wand and competing with singlesticks, and tumbling maidens in the rich shadows of the oak trees. There are booths where people sell pottery and posters, jewelry, weaving, and straw skimmers with ribbons that say, JAZZ—DO YOU DIG IT?; and there is a bar where you can watch the performers on closed-circuit TV, if you'd rather. Even the Sheriff of Nottingham and his henchmen seem to have become mellow and reasonable in recent years. The Monterey police chief fell in love with the hippies who flocked to a recent Folk Festival, sent all his men home, and accepted an invitation to visit the Haight-Ashbury. Support your local police.

We caught part of the tenth annual Jazz Festival: an afternoon of blues, beginning with the Clara Ward gospel group and going all the way through to Big Brother and the Holding Company, a San Francisco rock band. It was a hot, clear September Saturday, and there must have been five thousand people at the Fairgrounds. The hippies, real and plastic, set the tone of things, with their gowns and serapes, and the iridescent cars and trucks parked all around. Yet there weren't that many of them—there never are. It's just that we see them and think about them, as we never think about the others—the slacks and shirtsleeves and sports coats that we meet.

The Clara Ward Singers were handsome ladies in dark, spangled dresses, who sang and shouted and beat their tambourines, and went off into skittering little tap steps; all with flawless professionalism, and a certain cold timing. I saw them at the Village Gate years ago, and they were the same way then.

T-Bone Walker came on after them, and then B. B. King. It was a subtle, haunting choice of blues guitarists. T-Bone and King have the same roots—the country blues, sung in Chicago and Detroit by people who still remember the country. Both men sing about women and poverty; but T-Bone Walker is still the country blues—the voice lining it out, four bars at a time, the guitar repeating and mocking and affirming; and B. B. King is different, closer to modern jazz and modern rock music. He uses his guitar like a saxophone (he sings like a sax as well), which is something the white rock groups do now, having picked it up from the Negro rhythm-and-blues bands by way of the English. That's called cultural cross-fertilization.

Dead Cypress, Carmel

King invited T-Bone back after he played his own set, introducing him as "that wonderful guy who's still the best on the guitar." It was a winner's gesture, for B. B. King is deservedly on his way up to the big clubs and the big record contracts; while T-Bone Walker is back scuffling, playing the ghetto bars and the blind pigs, riding buses between Houston and Nashville and Chicago, playing wherever people still want to hear the blues. The two of them played briefly together, but it wasn't especially good.

Where we sat in the grandstand, most of the people around us were middle-aged Negros. The two men just behind us talked quietly as T-Bone Walker and B. B. King played, remembering other times and places when they had listened to the blues. They knew every song; they were part of the deep sound of recognition that went up with the first phrase of each song. King and T-Bone still had something to say to them, and Monterey wasn't so far from Chicago that they couldn't hear it.

In the row ahead of us, between an older Negro couple and a skinny, well-dressed white boy, sat Elrene. I know her name because she told it to me. She told everyone her name. Elrene was twenty-five or twenty-six. She had a laughing, tumbly-soft kind of face, and her skin was the color of sage honey. Elrene wore a tight blue dress with white polka dots the size of hockey pucks, and she drank gin and tonic all afternoon. It was impossible not to look at her, or to look at her without smiling. When she caught you smiling, she smiled back and told you her name.

Next, unexplainably, came the Gary Burton Quartet. They weren't scheduled for the Festival at all, and neither Liberace nor the Austrian Tonkuenstler would have been more out of place in a blues program. They weren't bad, but they should have been playing indoors, in the dark, for a hundred silent people who stayed in their seats. At Monterey, people walk around and make noise. They do listen to the music, and react to it, but as part of the setting for themselves on a beautiful day. They aren't about to be the background for the music. Some jazz was never meant to catch this shifting, tricky rapport, but some music was born of it.

The Gary Burton Quartet worked away, dimly visible through their self-absorption, and the man sitting behind us said sadly to his friend, "What is this? I don't dig this." But they both applauded earnestly when the guitar or the vibes got off a solo.

Elrene leaned back toward my wife. "Are you having fun? That's good. Always have fun, wherever you are, that's the way I feel about it. If people like you, well, fine, that's beautiful—and if they don't, that's fine too. Just go on your way and have fun, and accept the things you can't change. And what you *can* change—leave it alone! *Don't* mess with it!" And Elrene looked around at everyone who was smiling at her, and she laughed.

Then Big Brother and the Holding Company came on. They aren't the best of the rock bands, to my ear, or the most original. But they have a sound, somewhere between the blues and (I swear!) the old Paul Whiteman hootchy-kootchy thing; and they have Janis Joplin. She's a plain little Texas girl who sings like a goddam maniac, dancing and shaking herself into a frenzy, swinging her body like a wild bell. She screams and snarls most of her songs, but when she did "Bye-bye, Baby," her voice was low and rich, perfectly controlled, with a marvelous cutting edge. This one will last, however the music changes. That edge is there.

Everyone was dancing, even the people who just stood on the benches in the grandstand, clapping and watching the dancers down below among the folding chairs. Chains formed and went hopping up and down the aisles, sometimes behind hippies in beads and feathers and fringes; sometimes led by dumpy girls wearing sorority sweatshirts and Bermudas, and those silly straw hats. Wherever you turned your eyes, there was a sudden bright eddy as some little girl went away into her own crazy dream. It was like those three or four of the Mary Poppins stories that end with fairy tales dancing together; or shadows, or constellations; or sea creatures dancing the hornpipe on the ocean floor.

Some of them were high, surely—you could smell the grass—but most of it was the music. A lot of right-wing fundamentalists believe that rock music is a Communist plot, aimed at subverting our youth by a kind of mass hypnosis: harnessing their heartbeats to a single vast rhythm, which could then somehow be directed against all that we hold dear. They're almost right, that's the funny thing. Everyone in the Fairgrounds belonged to that beat, and so, for a while, to Big Brother and the Holding Company, to Janis Joplin. But they belonged a little to one another, too—and that's really what rock is all about, and group therapy, and Utopian communities, and all the other foolishnesses by which a peculiarly lonely people try to find their way to some unstudied kindness and affection. I don't think the Kremlin's going to be able to do much with that. They don't know how to handle it at home.

Elrene was dancing all over as she stood there, her bottom going like a basketball caught up in a fast break. Each time she clapped, her fingers bounced on her palm like brushes on a snare drum. "Where's your *soul*?" she cried to the skinny boy, and he grinned in some embarrassment. He was clapping too, but it wasn't the same thing, and I felt for him. I've been in the same position, doing my best.

In the rear aisle, a shirtless boy was dancing slowly with a girl wearing a curious cross between a purple leotard and a lace doily. A large, red-bearded man reached down to Elrene, and she caught his hand and came swinging over the benches, laughing in her polka-dot dress. On the way up, she stopped beside us and said, "I'm Elrene. Are you enjoying yourselves?" She was very drunk, but on her it was sweet and gracious, as though she were the hostess for the whole afternoon.

"Sock it to me!" she sang as we shook hands, and then she was off with the redbeard. On stage, Janis Joplin was finishing up the last number so it would stay finished.

> "*And it feels*
> *like a ball-l-l-l*
> *a-a-a-a-nnd chai-ai-ai-ain!*"

As she wrung out the last notes, one of the guitarists—suddenly overcome by it all—began to wrestle with his amplifier. He won, but the thing put up a good, sullen fight before he finally hauled it down in a spat of smoke. This is becoming obligatory in big rock performances these days. An English group called The Who generally end by destroying all their instruments. Come right down to it, I don't really trust spontaneity as much as I did. The market's too good.

But it was a fine day, and I sure liked Elrene. I hope she got home all right. I hope she reads this.

Carmel, six miles from Monterey, has been a resort for sixty years, since people like Mary Austin and Goerge Sterling were living in cabins in the woods. In this case, the historic pattern reversed itself—Carmel's no place for hungry writers now. I don't like Carmel much, and I'm quite aware that this isn't at all fair. It's a pretty town, and most commendably preserved and protected against all the forces that cut down trees, muddy the air, foul the water, and turn meadows into gas stations. I can't even use my old argument that Carmel would be a very bad place to be poor. There are no poor people in Carmel.

Carmel Mission

Anyway, it's pretty. There are lots of shoppes and snuggeries, cozies and quaintsies; pleasing cottages, wonderful virgin oaks, and a Bach Festival in the summer. Ah, I don't know what I expect from Carmel. The good people have done everything possible to keep things just the way I like them, and still I bitch. I just wish that it didn't cost so much for towns to be pretty, and that a pretty town could still stay alive.

Couple of nice things. The Mission San Carlos Borromeo is nearby, and it's probably the most beautiful one of all. It looks Moorish—an excellent thing in a mission. Point Lobos is here too, and this is a good place. Stevenson is supposed to have modeled Spyglass Hill on this country. And in Carmel itself, on a side street off Ocean, which is the main drag, there is a little old lady who sits in her second-story apartment and makes fudge. I don't remember the name of the street, but it's a left turn as you walk down towards the beach, and she has a sign out. It is fudge from Fudgeville.

But the really good thing about Carmel is that if you go a little way past it and take the Carmel Valley road, you can visit Ira Sandperl and Joan Baez at their Institute for the Study of Nonviolence. I met Ira and Joan in the summer of 1966, when I wrote about the institute for a magazine. It's a year later now.

The institute is just beyond Carmel Valley Village: a low, white building with a tile roof, set a little way back from the road. Joan Baez bought it two years ago. She set up the school originally to give Ira a place to live and instruct her — and anyone else who wanted to hear what Ira had to say—in the principles of Gandhian pacifism, *satyagraha*. In actual practice, this means that Ira is a lovely, sensible man, and God knows few of them ever get a chance to talk to a lot of people. He does talk about Gandhi at the institute, but he talks about a lot of other things as well—though they usually turn out to be Gandhi too.

The track of this bad year is clear and deep on Ira. He's shaved off his beard ("to give me a fifteen-second start when I'm talking to television people"), and his face looks as though every headline has marched across it. The stoop is more pronounced; so is the gauntness, and the foot that dragged slightly drags more now. But he's still Ira. He put his arms around me when we met this time, and kissed me.

Ira Sandperl

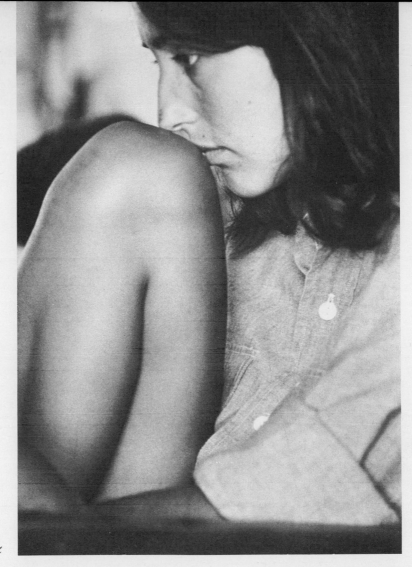

Joan Baez

He lives downstairs, entirely surrounded by books. It's funny—I bought books from Ira in the days when he worked part time at Kepler's in Palo Alto. I didn't know who he was then, or who I was, and I paid even less attention than I do now. That was seven years ago. Now he and Mike (who was in Cuba then) and I are sitting on the floor in his room, drinking beer, and we really are friends. It's like a long, slow dance.

The last year, strangely, has been a good one for the institute. Local opposition—instant and visceral, as most reactions to Joan Baez are, one way or another — has faded almost entirely; and the idea of the institute was greeted so enthusiastically when Joan and Ira toured Europe that they are planning to open a school in Paris and one in Rome, as well as in New York and Chicago.

Then there is the recent alliance with Martin Luther King, born during the integration riots in Grenada, Mississippi. (This interview was conducted in the fall of 1967, months before the assassination of Dr. King and Joan Baez's marriage to David Harris.)

Ira and Joan will be raising money for the Southern Christian Leadership Conference, and helping to lead the demonstrations and acts of massive civil disobedience that are the pacifist's only weapon. Ira himself is of two minds about this.

"Martin's in a terrible bind just now. He's trapped between Roy Wilkins and Stokely Carmichael, and he's sad and confused because he thinks he's failed. But he's the only man we can work with — he's the only one who still gives a damn about nonviolence, and who realizes that bopping people on the head is what keeps anything important from ever really changing. I don't know if we'll turn out to be any good to each other, but it's worth a try."

The pattern of the sessions at the institute is still the same: there are three during the summer, and they usually run for two or three weeks. There are occasional weekend sessions in the fall. The students pay a fee that covers their room and board at a guest ranch across the road. From one to five every day, they sit in a big, clean, bare room and talk with Ira about nonviolence.

"Of course, I always do most of the talking," he says. "I hear this middle-aged wind-bag, this weary peacenik, going on and on, and I wish somebody would interrupt him, for God's sake — argue with him, contradict him, put him down, shut him up. But they hardly ever do. Almost all of them are on my side to begin with, or they think they are. The ones I'd like to get are the SDS kids, the Black Power people, the ones who take ROTC and join fraternities. I don't mind saying the same stupid things over and over, but sometimes I do get a little tired of saying them to the same people."

Ira's position is summed up very well in one of his favorite sayings: "You don't get to kill the bad guys." This has never been a popular attitude, but it used to get a fair amount of support from battered minorities trying only to stay alive in a world run by bad guys. But in this particular time, which has seen the Vietnamese, the Algerian FLN, the Angolan rebels, the Israelis, and the dozen Cubans of the Sierra Maestra stand up success-fully against large numbers of bad guys, the insulted and injured are coming to look on nonviolence as pitifully irrelevant; or as another mask for United Fruit and the CIA. Gandhi's philosophy makes very few headlines these days, even in India.

But Joan Baez does. There is about her a sense of a paid-for honesty that somehow gives legitimacy to whatever she becomes concerned with — a song or a belief — and makes it seem something worth concern. Everyone who has a song or a belief ready for market wants Joan Baez to lay her hands on it. Legitimacy is no rarer today than it ever was, but the need of it is more conscious.

Joan is Ira's wedge, his way in, connecting him with a far larger and more varied audience than his unfashionable, unmarketable philosophy could ever gain him alone. Whoever wants Joan's presence has to take Ira too; a situation which continues to amuse Ira very much. Half his life has been spent in the peace movement, and his sense of irony is in excellent shape. "And now, a word from our sponsor," he likes to say. "Let's hear it for draggy old Uncle Ira and his nonviolence thing."

Ira's daydreams have grown a little desperate with the desperate year. He has an idea about bringing Dr. King and Pope Paul together to present a program for social reform in Latin America; and at one point he was making a half-serious attempt, through her confessor, to persuade Jacqueline Kennedy to go to Vietnam. But he has no illusions. "Joan said it best a while back. Nonviolence has been a terrible, absurd, utter failure, no question about it. The only thing that's been more of a failure is violence."

He tells a story — Ira is one of the great storytellers — about two awkward young men who visited him at the school recently. "They started off by saying, 'Mr. Sandperl, you probably hate us — ' and I said, 'I don't know yet. Give me a reason to hate you.' So they showed me their Marine dogtags. I said, 'No, that's not a good enough reason. If you've burned down a village or something lately, then maybe we can talk business.' Well, they don't want to burn any villages, but they aren't sure they want to go to jail either. 'Tell us what to do, Sandperl.' I said, 'I don't tell people to go to jail. I've been there lots, and it's no fun. If you *have* to go to jail, you'll know without asking me. Meanwhile, let's talk.'"

He looks at his big gold pocket watch and stands up; it's time to meet the class. "Things like that keep happening — enough to keep me going, anyway. I still have hope, but I'm not optimistic." Then he breaks up into that mad Ira giggle, as though absurdities were pelting him from all sides faster than he could get his breath. "Hell, I must be an optimist. I'm a forty-four-year-old Jew, and I'm alive."

There are about twenty students in the big room upstairs: more girls than boys, all under twenty-five. Many of the boys have long hair, but none of them are hippie types. From the outside, they seem like earnest, intelligent, attractive people, who, as Ira has said, don't really need to be talked out of dropping napalm on human beings. What the institute most needs is a resident Young American for Freedom, or to offer some sort of George Wallace Fellowship.

It's good to see her. She seems paler than she was last year, and more relaxed; as though that startling sealskin tan had worked down through her skin, warming and easing her. The thin shoulders are still tense, but she moves more happily, and she looks happy. I had forgotten how pretty her hands and feet are.

"How's the book going?" It isn't to be a novel, but a box of whatever she has, as Steinbeck says in the dedication of *East of Eden*. She smiles.

"It's about two-thirds done. It's going slowly, but I like it so far." That girl's smile must be part of some natural cycle of the earth, like the tides or the equinoxes, or animals growing their winter coats.

The meeting begins. Ira is trying to discuss this session's text, *A Sign for Cain*, by Frederic Wertham, but only a few of the students have enough of a grip on the book to argue about it. The talk wanders smokily off to draft resistance, to what Rap Brown said, to Ardrey's *African Genesis*; to the question of whether the North Vietnamese should have resisted the bombers and the Marines; to the native American violence that is reflected equally in our night streets and our foreign policy. It all needs to be talked about, but it's invariably one or two timewasters who do most of the talking, and they don't even know the words. They spend the greater part of the time defining terms.

"*And all the time,*" as the poem runs, "*Death beating the door in.*" Ira and Joan guide and shape and goad the conversation — she is better at it than he is, being less patient with timewasters and amiable foolishness — but in the end they wind up telling stories. Ira tells the wonderful one about the man who held him up in San Francisco, and how they finally had dinner together ("I said, 'Well, you pick the place, it's your three bucks'"); and the story of the Jain whose reverence for life extended to the microbes he might inhale when he breathed — but not as far as Pakistanis. "Some Jain *he* turned out to be!" Joan tells stories about Dr. King's lieutenant James Bevel, and his all-purpose "Sambo shuffle." She's a natural clown, though it rarely gets into her music.

Ira is getting ready to catch a plane to San Francisco, so Joan takes over for the rest of the session, holding the gold pocket watch in her lap. She talks of her own experiences with violence, and about her belief that the nonviolent person is much less vulnerable than his attacker. "You talk to them, always talk to them. The moment you make any sort of human contact, it cuts in half the number of people who are really willing to bash you. In Grenada we learned that it was important to keep talking to the troopers — otherwise, they stood around in little groups, giggling like kids, daring each other. But when one of us just walked up to a cop and asked him what time it was, suddenly he'd be at a terrible loss. He had to be human too, for maybe ten seconds. A lot of the time, that's all it takes."

And all the time, Death beating the door in. Even the hippies are carrying bicycles chains these days, and the cops have everything but the bomb. Gentle, hopeful friends expect civil war within the next few years. Serious people are talking about concentration camps. I suddenly hear myself saying, "But where are you going? You still seem to be trying to find a philosophical justification for nonviolence, which isn't necessary any more. Where are you going, what are you planning to do. What comes next?"

Joan turns to me. Okay, forget it. I don't want to make trouble. I'm with you. But she says calmly, "I'm not sure what you mean. We're not really trying to work out a program here, or a plan of action. We talk to people about living without violence, and we hope it makes enough sense to them that they'll go home and change their lives, whatever they decide to do about Vietnam, or Alabama, or their own families. There are a lot of things people can do. Ira and I are involved with a group in San Francisco who have decided that they won't pay the part of their income tax that goes to the military. I'm not sure — is that what you want to know?"

She hesitates, and then goes on in a sudden quiet rush. "Look, I know this is all futile. I don't have the slightest hope of making a difference, of changing the course this country is on. I just feel that it's better to be doing this futile thing than some other futile thing, or to be doing nothing at all."

Ira comes in near the end of the class, looking very respectable and rather subdued in a neat black business suit. He has come to say good-by before he leaves for the city. "I'll probably be back late tomorrow," he says. "You'll have to run things again, Miss Baez."

Joan bows as she gives him back his gold watch. "The day will be devoted entirely to talking about you. We ought to make it a regular thing, one Sandperl day in every session."

Looking at the faces around Ira — Joan's face as much as the others — I remember that he has always fought to keep from becoming a father figure at the Institute: the wise, kind, strong guru, so much in demand these days. But right now, as he sits there in his black suit, with his *yarmulke* of graying hair, they are all his children, and there's nothing he can do about it. And he knows it. The admission is there in his face too, just for this moment.

One of the young men mentions diffidently that he got beaten up this morning. Six teen-age boys jumped him as he was walking to the school.

"What did you do?" Ira asks, speaking with concern and the professional interest of a man who has been hit a lot.

"I fell down," the young man says. "Then I rolled down the bank and got away that way."

"Very good," Ira says. "See, there's one of the practical problems of *satyagraha*. What the hell to do when they really hit you."

Arts and Artists

I don't know what else is going on in Santa Barbara, but the junior high school band there is better than any high school group I've ever heard.

San Francisco Mime Troupe

Street scene, San Francisco Western Addition

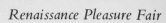

Poet and Friend

Happening to Rock Music, San Francisco

A trailer resort at the Salton Sea. This is a strange, rather sad place. I've wanted to
see it since I got hooked on the Colorado River as a child, and read all about the flood of 1905,
when the river burst through a faulty canal entry to inundate part of the Imperial Valley
for two years. Since the war, the Salton Sea area has grown steadily as a recreational and
retirement attraction for Southern Californians. Lots are selling well on the north
and west shores; a state park has been established; there is a new marina, and the sea has
been stocked with mullet and corvina. Five-hundred-mile power-boat races are held
here in November, and experimental models are tested all year round. The sea has even developed
a very respectable pollution problem — undeniable evidence of its successful urbanization.

But it seems like an awfully dreary place to retire to. The land around the Sea is stony
and unwelcoming, and few people have built on their lots; most have simply hauled up trailers
and plugged them in. Off the water, there isn't much to do. People grow small gardens,
or collect desert glass and antique bottles and make things like this bottle tree with them. No
trailer is without a TV antenna.

In a bar — shiny half-beams and vinyl seats, jukebox, pool table, bags of peanuts and
cashews, funny cards about credit and fishermen: here, nowhere — five or six men sit talking
very slowly. They are dressed like outdoorsmen, but their faces are soft and their eyes
colorless and puzzled. For an hour they talk about nothing but the last big wind (dangerous,
inexplicable storms often come up on the sea without warning), and about different
kinds of antennas and the best way to adjust them for good reception. They sound like women.

4. "Mr. Hearst Had a Great Sense of Humor"

(SAN SIMEON)

At San Simeon, William Randolph Hearst's castle — the greatest of the seven he owned — has attracted one million tourists since it was made part of the state park system in 1957. You ride a bus six miles up Hearst's "Enchanted Hill," landscaped with cypress, olive, plum, pine, and literally a score of other sorts of trees, none of which were there before Hearst was; sometimes sighting herds of zebra and hartebeest, which aren't native to the region either. The tour includes the grounds, the gardens, one of the three minor palaces, and either the ground floor or the upper floor of the main house. The upper floor costs more.

There isn't much to say about the place itself, without sounding like a catalogue or a souvenir brochure. It has to be seen, if for no other reason — and I think there really is no other reason — than for the strange, touching light it casts on William Randolph Hearst, and on the part of American that he spoke for and acted out. It isn't so much that he collected all this *stuff*: the paintings and tapestries and rugs; the statues and the fountains; the panelings, the rooms, the entire buildings taken apart in Greece and Italy and England, and reassembled here on this reassembled hillside in California. The sheer quantity and size of things numbs the imagination, and makes considerations of beauty impossible and irrelevant; but that's not the important point either. Plenty of Renaissance and Byzantine princelings must have grabbed out in exactly the same way, with the same blind hunger; acquiring, like Hearst, hundreds and thousands of art objects that they never saw, and never knew they owned. (One thinks of the Nazis in the last months of the war, desperately smuggling their stolen paintings and statues around Europe in boxcars.) The scope may have varied, but the hunger is familiar.

But Hearst is the one who really tried to live with it; to incorporate it *all* into his own life; to synthesize a world in which Jacobean bedrooms, baroque towers, palm trees and caged tiges, Spanish cloisters, Greek nudes and Italian terra-cotta madonnas, medieval Sienese banners and American ketchup bottles in a Renaissance refectory, could all fit together and be used. I can't help sympathizing with this wish to make all those old bought things as much your own, as much alive to you, as though you had earned them. I have it myself.

San Francisco Ballet

San Simeon

Hearst is dead, and there can't be many people who possess a will strong enough and greedy enough to make his world coherent for themselves. It must be wearing to work here. The girl who leads one particular downstairs turn doesn't like the place at all. I don't know how I know that — it's not in anything she says or does. It's the way she walks around those Graces and madonnas, and the tone in her low, nice voice when she answers questions. Mike said something once about park rangers being exactly the wrong sort of people to tie down to tours and lectures. She can't make anything personal out of this untied sprawl of wealth, and it shows.

But there's a middle-aged caretaker in La Casa Grande who's having a great time. He tags along with the tour when it comes indoors, zeroing in on stragglers who wander irregularly, hearing the guide's heavy words as though she were speaking a foreign language. As she discusses a classical Florentine portrait in the refectory, he whispers to me, "That's not the best of its kind, that's nothing. Stick around when they go out of the room, and I'll show you the best portrait in the place."

The tour moves on, and he eagerly beckons me over to a small, badly lighted painting of a seated man dressed as a primate of the Church. It doesn't look much like a seventeenth-century Italian work; there's a Spanish immediacy to the face, a realism perhaps half-intended. It's a very good painting.

"Gentileschi," the caretaker says. "They say it's a Caravaggio, but it's not. The lighting's all different — see, if Caravaggio had done it, you'd have your relief here and here, and this whole area would probably be concealed. Caravaggio didn't have a school, so you can't really be sure about who learned what from him, but this is Gentileschi all right. Best thing he ever did. They don't know what they've got, sticking it off in a corner."

He accompanies me for the rest of the tour, not only through the castle but out into the grounds again, and down to the indoor swimming pool, surrounded by its preening marble images. ("All Roman copies of Greek work, of course, except for that one there. Maybe.") Outside, he loses something — never authority, but some edge of enthusiasm. He doesn't care all that much for sculpture.

But painting he knows. What seems to delight him more than anything is talking about technique: the superiority of dammar varnish to a solution of mastic in turpentine; Sienese and Florentine methods of handling gold leaf (he much prefers water gilding to oil size); what kind of brushwork to employ in painting with egg tempera; how to make an emulsion of casein that won't turn yellow on you; the fifteenth-century German use of wet-into-wet painting, and how the Flemish artists made their whites. He talks like an experienced restorer, and mentions having cleaned several of the paintings in the castle and the guest houses. "I'm going to have to get to work on that little Desportes pretty soon, and I'm not looking forward to it. He's got way too much siccative in there, and it's cracking to beat hell."

And yet, there's no real sense of painting having been part of his life until he came

Hearst Castle

here. I know very little about art, but I grew up around people who grew up painting, and the feeling is different. I wonder how recently he learned all this marvelous stuff that he unquestionably knows; and how he picked it up, and why. What if he got it out of books, or from listening to hundreds of visiting artists over the years — and what difference does it make? He's happy with something, whether it's the pure knowledge or the knowingness; and by now the two must be inextricably mixed up together. He's got a good thing going, and he's happy. I hope he's happy.

He tells stories about Hearst as we walk along. "The thing about Mr. Hearst that people don't realize was that he had a great sense of humor. He liked to have a good time. Charlie Chaplin didn't get along with him, but that was because Chaplin didn't have any sense of humor at all. That's the truth. Chaplin wanted everybody to take him dead seriously all the time, the great artist. Well, Mr. Hearst wasn't going to go for *that*. He just couldn't be bothered with Chaplin."

Did he really know the old monster? Most of his Hearst stories can be found in Swanberg's biography, including — almost word for word — the one about the art dealer Duveen selling Hearst three pieces of fifteenth-century majolica for $101,000, and then letting Hearst know that another buyer would give him a 10 per cent profit on the pottery; hoping in this way to guarantee that Hearst would cling fiercely to his purchase and never ask for a refund. "But Mr. Hearst, he just pondered about it for a little while, and then he said, 'Well, I guess I'll take that profit.' And Duveen had to pay up. Mr. Hearst didn't like it when people tried to take advantage of him."

It doesn't matter. It's as though William Randolph Hearst had built his never-finished castle by the sea, surrounded it with strange trees and strange animals, stuffed it like a *piñata* with pretties, and died, for no other purpose than to give this one man a place to stand and a person to be. Maybe it did happen like that. Swanberg says Hearst was a generous man, in his own way.

Lettuce pickers near Salinas. As far as I know, Cesar Chavez hasn't yet begun organizing the farm workers in this area, but it's interesting that the foremen are always extremely suspicious of strangers with cameras. They keep asking who you're really working for

5. Never the Same Again

(DELANO)

The part of the San Joaquin Valley that I know best — meaning that I've driven through it quite a few times — is the southern half, stretching from around Merced down to Bakersfield. I have buzzed up and down U.S. 99 until I recognize names like Madera and Selma, Tulare, Tipton, Earlimart, just as though they meant something to me. But of all the areas of California, I think this is the one that gives the least of itself away to the hurtling eye. There is nothing here for the tourist. You just drive on through.

Fresno, next eight exits. Motels and motels. Malaga. Fowler. The horizons fade off into that California haze, and only the oil towers stand up. MOBIL, three minutes, easy return to freeway. Between the towers grows all the stuff we memorized for reports on California's important agricultural products — alfalfa, barley, potatoes, and sugar beets, and the largest cotton crop in the world — but going down 99, it's all a low green and yellow smudge. There is no sky. The air just lies there on top of everything.

Kingsburg. Goshen. Fruit stands with nobody ever in them. Long, muddy crumbles of shacks, with people in them. The vineyards are showing up now: fields like cemeteries, full of stunted black crucifixes. Tagus. Pixley. Before the freeways, you had to drive through a place, whether you wanted to or not, and stop for the traffic signals, and look around at it a little. Now you pass a couple of green-and-white signs in half a minute, and that was the town, those signs were it, as far as you'll ever know; and whatever is happening a hundred yards down from that turnoff, you'll never know. Delano.

I turned off at that sign once, with Mike. It was over a year ago, six months after the strike in the grapes had broken out, and we were hoping to free-lance a story. The boys from *Newslife*, we called ourselves; the professionals, in their corduroy pants. We never sold the story, and we've never been back till now.

There are worse places. About twelve thousand people; a main street with two movie theaters, a couple of hotels, a lot of auto parts stores and a supermarket; a quiet, rather pretty residential section, with trees; and a Mexican-Filipino downtown old enough to have developed its own tiny middle class. It is a processing and shipping town, too properous to give off that smell of shabby menace that clings to so many similar towns in the South or the Midwest. After Bakersfield, it's the most important city in Kern County.

What has been happening here since September 8, 1965, is the most significant labor development that has taken place in California in a long time. Its implications are more than political: they go back almost two hundred years, and they reverberate beyond California to strange places like Rio Grande City, Texas; Mesquite, New Mexico; Wautoma, Wisconsin. Briefly, sketchily, and with no attempt at impartiality, this is the story.

Senora Zapata

California has a tradition as old as itself of cheap — even captive — labor that has quite a lot to do with the state's present eminence and unease. It began with the Indians who cultivated the mission crops, and who were later put to work on the great feudal haciendas that arose after the missions had been dispossessed. The Chinese were the first foreign laborers to be imported: they were brought over by the tens of thousands after California became a state, to work in the mines and lay down road beds for the railroads. In the 1870s, with the railroads completed and the gold gone, many Chinese went into the fields of the Central Valley, and they worked there until the Chinese Exclusion Act of 1882 cut off that particular supply of manpower.

The Japanese came next, but that didn't work out well. They seemed to have a natural tendency to form unions, and they were probably the first of the California field workers to stage strikes. But after the Mexican Revolution broke out in 1910, thousands of peasants began crossing the border illegally to follow the crops up and down California and the American Southwest. The rise of modern "agribusiness" really begins at this point.

Mexicans were ideal for the California fields. There were lots of them; they could take the climate and the stoop labor; they had no history of organization, and their own basic tradition was one of submission to poverty and exploitation. Being here with the silent connivance of the state and federal governments, they had no security against deportation; and however little the California growers paid them, it was more than they could possibly make in Texas or Mexico. And they cost almost nothing to maintain. If you gave them chicken coops to live in, they'd live in chicken coops; if you provided no shelter at all, they'd sleep in the fields — and glean them for their meals, if necessary. They were a godsend.

With the bottomless reserve of wetback labor keeping wages at an absolute minimum, great agricultural baronies — Hunt Foods and Industries, DiGiorgio Fruit, Schenley Industries, California Packing — sprang up from one end of the state to the other, and quickly became the richest sector of the California economy. They had their difficulties in the Depression, when the government cut back drastically on the number of wetbacks blinked across the river, to make work for the Dust Bowl migrants: the Okies and Arkies who turned out not to be quite as docile as the growers had gotten used to. The bitter, tearing struggle described in *The Grapes of Wrath* and *In Dubious Battle* was never decided, just as the Depression itself never actually ended. But the war came, and the new arrivals went off into the defense industry, along with many Mexican-Americans. The wetbacks returned to the fields.

During the war years, the U.S. and Mexican governments came to a formal agreement regarding the contracting of *braceros*, and the program was continued after the war. In 1951, Public Law 78 codified the agreement, making it apparently clear that Mexican nationals would be imported to help with the harvest only if enough American workers were not available. Somehow they never were. The growers pointed out, quite honestly, that nobody would work for the wages the were offering, under the conditions they provided, except happy-go-lucky Mexicans who didn't really mind. Public Law 78 was renewed steadily until the end of 1964. Then, for a variety of reasons, it wasn't renewed any more.

Thus, as 1965 began, the California farm worker, migrant or resident, remained almost entirely unaffected by the great labor reforms of the twentieth century. He had no union, and his right to bargain collectively was not guaranteed by the National Labor Relations Act. Benefits that workers in the industrial unions have come to think of as rights both natural and divine — minimum wages, pension plans, child labor provisions, medical care, grievance procedures, unemployment compensation — were in agriculture left entirely to the dispensation of the particular employer.

What all this translates to is the fact that an economy based largely on the kindness of strangers is an economy based on suffering. And nobody who could have done something did anything.

But the signs that unionism was at last coming to the fields had been clear since 1959, when the AFL-CIO formed the Agricultural Workers Organizing Committee. Three years later, a pleasant, soft-faced little man named Cesar Estrada Chavez established the National Farm Workers Association. Migrant agricultural workers have always been the most difficult of laborers to organize; but by 1965, both unions claimed memberships of several thousand. Schenley Industries cleared $17,000,000 that year, and paid a man named Guadalupe Aguilar $64.49 for 63 hours of work, after $40.64 had been deducted for "temporary insurance."

The Filipinos of AWOC walked out of the vineyards on September 8, and the NFWA followed them eight days later. The immediate cause of the strike was the fact that grape-pickers in the Delano area were being paid $1.10 to $1.20 an hour, while the few thousand remaining *braceros* were guaranteed $1.40 by the United States Government. But the true cause was two hundred years old.

They won. When Mike and I were first in Delano, not a single grower had yet succumbed to the picketing and the surprisingly well-organized boycotts; to the bad press and the expensive inefficiency of scab labor. But since then, both Schenley and DiGiorgio have signed contracts with the union (AWOC and the NFWA recently merged to become the United Farm Workers Organizing Committee), and other companies are slowly following suit. Some of the growers have recognized the union as a bargaining agent for the field workers; and however long the rest takes, the agricultural system of California will never be the same again.

They have won. They are still poor, and still on the picket line, but they have won. What happens now?

Labor in America hasn't even pretended to be a force for change in twenty years. Having elevated the white industrial proletariat into the middle class, the great unions are essentially as unconcerned with the black, the poor, the unskilled and exploited — with anything beyond their own — as Daddy Warbucks. Perhaps it was unfair to expect the AFL-CIO to reform society; but the fact is that big labor today wears George Meany's face, and it's not a nice face.

But Cesar Chavez has a very nice face; and Dolores Huerta — UFWOC's vice-president and chief negotiator — is downright beautiful; and the Mexicans and Filipinos of Delano have beautiful faces, full of old roads and plowed fields and dead cars melting into the rainy earth. And this is the most important thing, the faces.

The real strength of the Delano strikers has always lain in their faces. It is the strength that comes, to paraphrase Denise Levertov, from being members of one another. It is this that has brought a great many middle-class Anglos into the movement, working not only in Delano, but in the other states where melon pickers and cucumber workers are beginning to organize. American life is desperately, pitifully short of this kind of membership. Look at the faces.

Walter Reuther made a speech in Delano on the hundredth day of *la huelga*. He pledged aid from United Auto Workers, and said, "This is not *your* strike. This is *our* strike." But it isn't the UAW's strike. That's the whole thing.

There is an old man here named Tim Kelly. He came to America in 1905 and worked as a longshoreman until he retired at the age of sixty-five. Then he went to school and studied harmony and counterpoint. Now he teaches the children of the *huelgistas* how to play the recorder. He's been in Delano about ten weeks, and the kids are playing folk tunes and nursery rhymes in two-part harmony. They are also playing the chorale from Beethoven's Ninth Symphony. Tim Kelly is eighty-three years old, and next week he's taking some of the children up to Fresno to attend a recorder concert and workshop.

Hard to say how much has changed in a year. Money is still short, but people get fed; and the Union is meeting the payments on two house trailers which serve as medical and dental clinics. UFWOC has also recently acquired forty acres of land just outside the city limits. You see newer used cars parked around the strike kitchen and the Filipino Hall,

Delano Grape strikers

where the union meetings are held. The meetings still last three hours or more, especially if the Filipinos are running things. They love meetings. The faces still look good.

There are a lot of visitors in town now, because of the march. It is the Easter weekend, the first anniversary of the *peregrinación*: the 245-mile walk up U.S. 99 that ended in Sacramento on Easter Sunday. This celebratory march will end with the dedication of the new land, and there will be a *fiesta* in the evening.

The march begins from the Hall on Saturday afternoon. Two by two, we set off on the four-mile walk to the edge of town behind a guitar and an accordion; under the American flag and the Mexican flag, the banner of the Virgin Mary, and the black eagle of *la huelga*. I walk beside a stocky man wearing a double-breasted brown suit, gold-rimmed glasses, and a heavy mustache that seems to be dragging his head and shoulders down. His hair is still mostly black, but he looks about sixty years old. We talk a little.

"Is there much longer?" he asks often.

"*No, un poco, un poquito. Media hora, no mas.*" That becomes our standard interchange, like one of those thirty-year running gags on old radio shows. He won't speak Spanish to me, and I won't speak English unless I have to. I am famous on two continents for my skill at making an awkward situation even more so.

He's from Zacatecas, but he has lived almost entirely in the States since the thirties. He lived in Texas for a long time, and after the war he moved to California. He came to Delano five years ago, because his grandchildren are here.

"Is there much longer?" It's a hot day, and he walks slowly in lumpy, cocoa-colored shoes.

"*Media hora.*" Half an hour. We are crossing a wide street, heading out of town toward the city dump. A cop holds up traffic for us, beckoning fiercely, his expression grimly neutral. Looking back, I can see the parade swinging around a corner, straggling but seemingly endless. Delegation signs bob up and down under the eagle banners: Woodville, Porterville, Gilroy, Selma, Corcoran, Modesto, San Jose — even the Schenley and DiGiorgio ranches, as though these were separate city-states. I ask the man next to me if he went on the *peregrinacíon* to Sacramento.

"I walk some. I walk to Madera. Then my son come in his car."

Used-car dealers come out and stand under their own plastic pennants to watch the march go by. The Delano people don't look quite as hostile as they used to — they take pictures now. Most of the route leads through the Mexican-Negro section of town, and families crowd their tiny yards, waving. Children sit on the curb, or ride bikes alongside for a little way, staring at the children of the march.

"Much longer, you think?" We are passing into open country — grass and the highway and the telephone poles, nothing more. Some of the children are being carried now. I recognize a girl I saw last year: grotesquely fat, but with a lovely, womanly face. She was nursing an infant then; she has another one now. I'd say she's twenty-two, twenty-three.

"*Dígame, señor,*" I say to the old man. "*Es mayor — uh — con la huelga? Es muy diferente ahora para usted? Muy — mucho cambio?*" Is it very different for you since the strike? How has your life changed, in twenty-five words or less?

He blinks at me without answering. I'm not sure he even heard me. He's walking so slowly that he's actually splitting the march in two. I see Cesar Chavez up ahead, walking hand in hand with a little boy. I like Chavez. There's nothing of El Maximum Leader about him; he gives an impression of humor and sweetness, and toughness under the sweetness, and something else under the toughness. He's thirty-nine now. I wonder what he'll look like when he's George Meany's age.

Musing about this, I suddenly realize that the old man is talking to me. He is speaking Spanish now, quietly, but very swiftly.

I can't get it. My Spanish is all right for passionless conversations, but not for this, not for whatever he's telling me. I catch words: *cuarenta y tres — mi señora — en la uva, en la naranja, en la alfalfa — y ese contratista — como los perros — sin agua, sin luz — mi amigo Rafael — setenta y cinco la hora — setenta y cinco, comprendes?* The names of towns flash by — Woodlake, Poplar, Wheatland, Del Rey, Dinuba, Tulare, Yuba City — and there are other names that must be growers; and his best friend Rafael went back to Mexico. He had a daughter who died — I got that — *y el doctor me dice . . . .* No, it's gone again. He mumbles, and he seems to have lost a consonant with every tooth.

Well, I asked him and he told me. This long, rattling old train of towns and injustices, years and losses — this is what has happened to him in his life; and last spring he walked all the way to Madera before his legs gave out. I got some of it anyway. I understand a little of it, surely.

The new forty acres will have a clinic and a co-op garage built on it within the year, but today it is dusty and naked, except for a speaker's stand, draped in banners. Cesar Chavez is there, and Larry Itliong — the leader of AWOC until the two unions merged. I recognized Luis Valdez, the young founder of El Teatro Campesino: the strikers' brilliant cross between the Living Newspaper and the *commedia dell'arte*. There is a priest, to consecrate the land, and a man from the AFL-CIO.

The speeches are necessary — you look around at the signs and flags and the proud, hungry faces, and you realize that revolutions have to have speeches, legends, rituals, there's no other way — but dull and predictable, even Chavez's speech. I fidget and scuff, brooding about priests and union officials. One of the meaningful things to come out of *la huelga* is the deep schism of conscience it's shivered into the California clergy, Catholic and Protestant alike. The new debates about whether the church should become involved in social reform — even in revolution — really began here in Delano, though Alabama got the headlines and the death. The church may yet save its soul in the Delanos; and so may the AFL-CIO, I suppose, but I don't know. It's embarrassing to see this tall, balding, pale-haired guy speaking to those faces in that battered Chicago voice. I look around for the man I walked here with, but he's gone.

Then Luis Valdez speaks, and something goes slightly agley with the whole scene. Compared to the others on the stand, Valdez is a jaguar: stocky, dark-skinned, with a mobile, sardonic mouth under a *zapatista* mustache. He's an American-born graduate of San Jose State, who worked with the San Francisco Mime Troupe before he came to Delano. He begins by speaking in Spanish and translating himself every so often; but after a while he doesn't translate any more, and it isn't really necessary.

Valdez doesn't think the strike is Walter Reuther's strike at all. Nor does he want it ever to become Walter Reuther's strike. What Valdez is saying, with his words and his hands and his mustache, is what James Baldwin suggested (how wearily long ago?): that he has no desire to be integrated into a burning house. He dislikes America in all its manifestations — the same long shudder of disgust encompasses President Johnson and Howard Johnson, Ronald Reagan and Erich Fromm; Vietnam and Leisure World; Bennett Cerf, Lawrence Welk, and Batman, with the government of Mexico heartily thrown in. Luis Valdez is a nationalist, but the only country to which he gives his allegiance is *la raza*, the Mexican people. He doesn't want *la raza* to accept America, to assimilate into tract houses and bad food; to lose its soul in saving various others; to become American. "We are not like these people," he says with finality, "we are not like them."

Daisy Harvest

Oyster Farm, Point Reyes

California at Work

This is Lee. He works for the Lucas Lumber Company, in a very small Klamath River town called Seiad Valley. By comparison with Union or Arcata, Lucas Lumber is non-existent, but it's doing quite well cutting pine and Douglas fir on the northern edge of the Klamath National Forest. Chick Lucas employs about thirty men, many of whom are itinerants, following the timber to Oregon or Wyoming during the winter months. Some come back every year, and some never come back. ("Loggers are children, most of them," one of Chick's truckdrivers says without malice. "You got to take care of them like children.") But Lee is an old friend, who has worked with Chick for nine years.

Chick Lucas is in his early forties: a stocky, fair-skinned man who looks like a nice cop. He has been cutting trees since he was twelve years old, except for a period when he had a broken back and turned to farming and running a sawmill on the side. "In those days, in in the thirties," he says, "they didn't give a damn about anything except getting those trees down fast. If you got hurt, too bad; if you worked too slow, they'd get somebody else. It's different now. You have to be more considerate of people—that's the real change, not the new equipment. I spend half my time warning my men to slow down and be careful, not to hurt themselves."

They haven't been using axes and crosscut saws for a long time. Felling is done with power saws, and a portable tower called a "yarder" brings the logs snaking out of the woods on steel cables. (I remember them leaping into the air in a curious parody of the dune buggies.) Lee trims the logs, and a clawed machine lifts them onto a truck. It's hot, dirty, dangerous work, but strangely graceful. Men who don't move like bullfighters around the logs probably don't last very long.

The lumber industry has always figured in my mind as a faceless, immeasurably energetic villain; never more than temporarily balked in its aim of destruction—my equivalent, I guess, of other people's international Communist conspiracy. But here's Chick Lucas, who likes trees and wild country, and who enjoys his work quite apart from the money he makes at it. "I don't know what else I could possibly do. I talk to my wife about it sometimes, really trying to imagine." He's a good citizen, in the oldest sense of the word: when the Klamath flooded in 1964, Chick's machines worked for days opening the roads; and when there are forest fires, he goes out and helps to fight them. The fortunes of most of the people in his small realm are tied to his own, and whatever affects the great lumber barons—the bad guys—affects him. I think about him now, when I read the reports of another battle in the endless war between Our Side and Theirs. Allow the enemy so much as one human face, and you're in serious trouble.

The redwood mill at Scotia is the largest in the world, and the free catwalk tour of it is well worth taking. It should be part of every Californian's education to see how the half-ton streams of water batter the thick bark off a redwood log, and how swiftly and efficiently the band saws reduce it to slats and shavings. It's very subjective, of course, to say that a two-by-four is a reasonably dignified thing for a tree to become, and that a cigar box, a shiny tourist gimcrack, or a compressed-wood panel isn't, but there you are.

The really interesting thing about Scotia is that it is about the last of the company lumber towns, in which every foot of land, every house, and every facility belongs to the mill. There used to be dozens of such fiefs scattered through the lumber country of Washington, Oregon, and Northern California, and they were the scenes of some of the bloodiest battles in the history of the American labor movement. Today, the Pacific Lumber Company pays its workers in cash, instead of printing its own scrip, and generally compares to its pre-New Deal past as Sweden compares to Haiti. People wait for years to move into Scotia. But every once in a while, even now, you run into some old, punchy, boring Wobbly who wants to talk about the way it all was in 1911.

Digging irrigation channels in the Imperial Valley. This is the "Low Desert," the country lying south of the Mojave Desert, bordering on Arizona and Mexico. Much of the land is well below sea level. It's even hotter and drier than the Mojave, and three-quarters of it is barren, undeveloped southwestern wasteland. Yet the Imperial and Coachella Valleys, which have access to the Colorado River, are only outranked by the counties of the San Joaquin Valley in the total value of their agricultural commodities. Coachella is greener, given largely to orchards and vineyards, to long aisles of date palms, eucalyptus and tamarisk windbreaks; with golf courses as important a crop as any other. The Imperial Valley is all business, dusty and low to the ground. Truck crops, grown in the off-season, are the leading product here; then come feed crops, livestock, cotton, and sugar beets.

Water is the key, as it is throughout most of California. In the empty mesas that flank the Imperial Valley, a lone cow would be hard put to stay alive on cholla cactus and galleta grass; yet half a million head of cattle are not only raised in the Valley itself, but brought down for summer fattening when the rest of the state is yellow and brittle. The two Low Desert counties, Imperial and Riverside, draw almost all their water from the Colorado, via the Imperial Dam and the All-American Canal. But the river passes through six other arid states, and California's share of the Colorado was sharply reduced by a Supreme Court decision in 1963. Sea-water conversion may eventually replace the loss and permit further reclamation of the Low Desert.

General Sherman tree

6. Creatures so Vast that You Misunderstand Them

(KINGS CANYON TO YOSEMITE)

If you have time — not just time enough, but time to scatter like seeds — a very good thing would be to start at the Tehachapi Pass, or thereabouts, and go north, bearing east when in doubt. Turn left at the Oregon border, and head west until you come to the ocean. The roads of northernmost California are generally erratic, impractical, and unrecommended; take full advantage of them. Then make another left, and go down the coast as far as you care to. The coast is always good.

For me, the best of it is contained in this jagged, broken loop: the Sierra Nevada, the redwood coast, Sonoma and Mendocino and Marin, San Francisco, Santa Cruz; the road along the edge of the country that leads through the Monterey Peninsula and the Sur. This is California when I think happily of California. This is the California of my mind.

I don't know the Southern Prongs area very well. The country doesn't feel like part of the Sierra at all: it's in Kern County, and in the summer it looks as though a flange of the hot, bare, southern San Joaquin had been wrinkled into low brown mountains blotched with chaparral. The real Sierra begins at Mineral King, which is the southern tip of Sequoia National Park.

Mineral King will be starting to look different by the time this book comes out. Right now, it's a very small, quiet, secret sort of place. There are a few cabins for rent, and a lot of places to hike, and some people have been coming here for years. But Mineral King lies at the foot of slopes that would make a magnificent ski run, and that's what they're going to be, by the grace of the Walt Disney people. It'll be great for the Los Angeles ski buffs who spend their winter weekends driving a thousand miles to Squaw Valley and back. But I just discovered Mineral King this year, and I'm sorry to be losing it so soon. Well, that's California. That's that California feeling.

Sequoia and Kings Canyon are really one park, running sixty-five miles from end to end. The essential difference between them is that the General Sherman Tree is in Sequoia, and my heart is in Kings Canyon. That's one's mine.

In Sequoia we took a guided tour of Crystal Cave, which is a cold marble pocket, full of darkness that pushes against you; and of a strange, pointless beauty that goes well with paradoxes about trees falling in forests and the sound of one hand clapping. The walls drip their colors like melting candles, and the stream that runs through the cave is wax-white, ice-white, the color of anything that was born in the dark and lives in the dark. And the people who trudged after the ranger's lantern looked ugly in its light: fat and soft, almost malformed, as though the darkness had squashed them. They said very little to each other.

We saw a lot of the same people half an hour later, at the General Sherman Grove. They walked around taking pictures of the big trees — which is almost as silly as writing about them — and they laughed, and clowned with their children, and started conversations with strangers. There is a kind of beauty that rubs off on the people who behold it; or, rather, draws them into itself and makes them beautiful too. The sequoias are like that.

You can feel the life in them. It's the bark, partly: the bark of a *sequoia gigantea* is a couple of inches thick, practically fireproof; and yet it has a softness about it, a sense of skin, almost a furriness. The shape has something to do with it, too. The first limbs begin well over a hundred feet from the ground, and the tree has almost no taper; so the effect of being in a grove of sequoias is very much like standing among great animals — creatures so vast that you misunderstand them, as a kitten must think your hand or your leg is you.

They're tender too — like elephants — at once indestructible and surprisingly vulnerable. You mustn't step on their roots, which lie very near the surface of the ground, because that packs the earth closer around them and makes it hard for them to nourish themselves. Ironically, an occasional forest fire actually benefits the sequoias by burning off the brush and creepers that grow over their roots. They're very often struck by lightning, and the old trees whose crowns haven't been blasted and split usually start to die up there anyway. Yet they can be cut almost entirely through, or have eight-foot tunnels scooped through them, and live; they can be burned black, split in two, and live, and propagate at a rate directly related to the extent of their injuries. And when they do die, they lie without rotting for a long time, and often new trees are born from their bodies.

Curious, in a time when people are once again experimenting with the idea of the utopian community, to remember that a socialist settlement once existed here. It was called the Kaweah Co-operative Commonwealth Colony, and it lasted from 1886 till the early 1890's. The colonists were going to cut trees and quarry marble, plant orchards and vineyards, and live a good life independent of the system. They founded a town, built a road, started a newspaper, and had plans for a university. For those few years, the General Sherman was renamed the Karl Marx Tree.

But in 1890, an act of Congress created the Sequoia National Park, and though the colony then moved to private land within the park, it broke up messily a short while afterward. I'm beginning to believe that you can't get to Jerusalem from here, ever. You have to build it where you are.

Kings Canyon is a hell of a place. That's the area I want to explore when the children are a little bigger and I'm a little happier on a horse. It's high Sierra, wilder than Sequoia, with that almost shocking sense of granite that the lower country doesn't have. This is

Rock climbers, Yosemite

where the origins show through. The berry bushes, the dogwood, the lupine, even the sequoias themselves, begin to seem like a ragged, genteel veil over the reality of the rock. All I know of Kings Canyon at this writing is the road along the south fork of the Kings River, but the rock is there. It's black, and it's orange, and there are veins and splotches of green, and white scars. To sit here and look down at that fierce little river slicing along far below is frightening and peaceful at the same time. I like this stone place. I want to come back here.

Working up toward Yosemite, you have to dip back into the San Joaquin Valley for a little way, and it's a very instructive thing to do. You can see the valley sky long before you come under it, and after the sky of the high country it's like sticking your head under a smudgy, sweaty woollen blanket. Most air seems like that when you first come down from the Sierra. You get used to living and moving in it again quickly enough, but it becomes easier to understand the people who never do get used to it.

Chuck Pratt is one of these people. Chuck is a rock-climbing bum, as other men are ski bums or tennis bums. He lives in Yosemite about eight months of the year, and spends the rest of his time earning, at most, five hundred and ninety-nine dollars. Chuck has been living like this since he was seventeen. He is in his late twenties now.

"This is what I do," he says. "I really don't want to do anything else. I could probably get a good job and go climbing over the weekends, and on my summer vacation, but I'd rather go climbing all the time. Every once in a while, it does seem like a silly, meaningless thing for a grown man to be doing, but I suppose everybody feels like that at one time or another. It's no sillier than anything else, and I like it."

People have been climbing in Yosemite since Congress granted the valley itself to California in 1864, creating the first of the state parks. The surrounding wilderness — the valley occupies seven square miles out of 1189 — became a national park in 1890, and California gave the valley back a few years later. All the high summits — Starr King, Broderick, the Lost Arrow, the Cathedral Spires, and the great granite monoliths like Half Dome and El Capitan — have long since been mastered; and Yosemite has more of the feeling of Valhalla than of Mecca. One of my oldest friends is a climbing nut who sees countries and continents from eight or ten thousand feet above sea level. I think he fully expects to come to Yosemite when he dies, and begin to live the way Chuck Pratt does. It's a good life, or afterlife — either way, it makes more sense than most.

Mike and I were in Yosemite in April, when the snows were melting and Bridalveil Fall was bending down too heavily for the wind to play with it. The mountaineering season wouldn't really begin for more than a month — even Chuck hadn't been back for very long — but there were twenty or thirty climbers in Camp Four that weekend, practicing on boulders, tying knots over and over, and laying out their hardware: pitons, crampons, carabiners. Two men were already on El Capitan, halfway up the hard, sleek face after three days.

I like climbers. As a group, they seem very friendly and open, even if they don't talk about anything else. When I mentioned this to Chuck, he answered, "They aren't competing with each other, for one thing. Climbers have to help each other — not just within the team, but anybody who needs to know something you know. You might save somebody's life by showing him a better way of belaying, or teaching him how to detect crevasses under the snow. There aren't any secrets in climbing, and there isn't any big status thing about it. People mostly just climb for the sake of climbing. Maybe that's what makes the difference."

The relationship between the climbers and the management of Yosemite is, at best, uncomfortable. Camp Four is unofficially set aside for the climbers' use, but they say that the ten-day limit is much more strictly enforced against them than it is against the tourists and the fisherman. Park authorities claim in turn that the climbers shoplift in the stores and steal firewood from the rangers' supply. Both charges, according to Chuck, are occasionally true.

"But I don't think that's the real reason they're down on climbers," he says. "I think it's that climbers don't consume very much. It's not like skiing, where you have a whole superstructure of things you can sell to skiers. Lessons, clothes, equipment, lodges, lift fees, and that *après-ski* mystique, which was just invented to sell drinks. But rock-climbing

Yosemite Valley

doesn't benefit anybody except the people who actually do it. And Yosemite is a pretty commercial place, in its own way."

Most of the climbers we met were students on vacation, and a good half of them came from other states. In the evening they crouched around a good stolen fire and talked about bergschrunds and *séracs*, moraine and scree; cornices and icefalls and marginal crevasses; pitches, verschneidungs, laybacks, rappelling, glissading, Prusiking. They argued about technique — English asceticism as opposed to German reliance on mechanical aids — ideal rope thicknesses; nailed boots against hard rubber soles, woollen longies against flannel; personal methods of keeping snow out of your boots. Chuck spoke often of a man named John Salathé, who climbed alone, and who developed a revolutionary technique of belaying himself through his own pitons. It was jargon, surely, but it didn't have the dulling, segregative effect that jargon usually has on me. I listened, and when I asked how you Prusiked, somebody told me.

I asked Chuck why he climbed, and he told me that too, but there's not much point in setting it down. Everybody uses the same words to explain his love.

"Do you think you'll be doing this in ten years, twenty years?" *There's* the American question: When are you going to quit having fun and settle down to the serious business of doing something you don't like? But that's what most of these kids will be getting around to in a sadly short time. Chuck will be here when they've all gone home. Besides, I always want to know where everybody will be in a few years. Not me — never me — but everyone else.

"Somewhere else, probably. I'll have about climbed Yosemite out in another ten years. But I'll be climbing, I'm sure of that. It's what I do. It makes me happy."

As for Yosemite itself, I'm not going to write much about it. Read John Muir.

What makes me awkward about Yosemite is the thing that makes it unique among all the wildernesses I have seen: not its physical beauty, but a sense of wholeness. The valley was scoured out of a single stone by the glaciers, like those strange, lacy worlds, full of spaces and objects, that people carve within a piece of wood or ivory or soap; and Yosemite feels like a complete world, to be known. Muir knew it — it belonged to him. It belongs to Chuck Pratt, and to Ansel Adams, and to a lot of other people whose names I don't know. It doesn't belong to me, and I don't think it ever will. I'm bad and greedy and sad about all worlds that don't belong to me.

Kings Canyon, though. I have a feeling that that place hasn't really been known by too many people yet. It might be easy to love Kings Canyon.

As far as I know, the coyote is the only wild American mammal that has actually extended its range since the coming of the white man. This one had stopped traffic on the Tioga Pass road out of Yosemite, and was hurrying back and forth having its picture taken. It ate everything that was thrown from the cars; peels, rinds, and wax paper making no neverminds. Doubtless, on such a diet, it must have had a weight problem, a vitamin deficiency and a dangerously high cholesterol count, but it was a handsome, rich-furred coyote anyway, and very calm. You could get within ten feet of it before it began easing away.

Alpine County

7. Places Nobody Wants

(ALPINE, MODOC AND THE NORTH)

The main road out of Yosemite on the east takes you over the Tioga Pass and into LeeVining, where it joins U.S. 395, the big highway that goes all the way into British Columbia. This is the Forelands, the northern tip of the Trans-Sierra region — that odd, naked, empty edge of Nevada that somehow belongs to California. It begins at the southern end of Lake Tahoe, and ends in Death Valley.

It's all dry sagebrush and bunch grass country, but the Forelands is less so than the rest of the Trans-Sierra. There's a grim little joke about that. The Forelands is ranch land now, as it was during most of the nineteenth century. But some water does come down from the high mountains, and by the 1890's there was a fair amount of irrigation farming going on. Market towns cropping up in the Owens Valley; a reservoir planned for the Owens Gorge; four times as much land under cultivation as there is now. Great hopes.

Then they built the Los Angeles Aqueduct, and that was the end of that. The Aqueduct supplies two thirds of Los Angeles' water, and the Forelands is cattle and sheep country again. Most of the farmers pulled out during the Depression, leaving a few groves of willow trees behind them. The population has grown with the tourist trade, but there are still only about 15,000 people in the whole Trans-Sierra. And very little water.

Mono Lake doesn't count. Mark Twain talks about Mono Lake in *Roughing It*.

> . . . *It is an unpretending expanse of grayish water, about a hundred miles in circumference, with two islands in its center, mere upheavals of rent and scorched and blistered lava, snowed over with gray banks and drifts of pumice-stone and ashes, the winding-sheet of the dead volcano, whose vast crater the lake has seized upon and occupied.*

Actually, it's quite pretty in its own way — blue and silver when the sun shines straight down, with a kind of purple feeling about things in the afternoon, especially around the chain of volcanic craters on the far shore. But the great man was quite right about the general nature of the place. It's as barren as the Dead Sea, and even more alkaline — its water holds about twenty different chemicals in solution — and it is much given to violent, soapy storms that pile the shores with drifts of burning lather. Twain warns, "This water is not good for bruised places and abrasions of the skin," and tells that story about the raw dog that jumped into the lake to get away from the flies.

Bodie

" . . . He was not a demonstrative dog, as a general thing, but rather of a grave and serious turn of mind, and I never saw him take so much interest in anything before. He finally struck out over the mountains, at a gait which we estimated at about two hundred and fifty miles an hour . . . "

This region had its own, less-familiar Gold Rush that began as the Mother Lode was running dry, and lasted a good deal longer. Gold was first discovered in the Mono country in 1852, but the great strike was made in Aurora, which is actually in Nevada — although this fact wasn't established until Aurora had become the county seat. But the boom times, the wild years, came in the late 1860s and early '70s. And the wildest of the camps, and the very last to die, was Bodie.

Bodie is north of Mono Lake, about halfway to Bridgeport. A bad road runs east through red and yellow hills to take you there. When you come over the last rise and see Bodie, stop and look at it for a moment before you go on down.

It's a very small town, sprinkled between two of the low, bare hills, and it's all one color from a distance — brown, the brown of a dead leaf. Live wood holds light, but Bodie stays the same color as the sun moves. The only shininess comes from the huge old mill and mine above the town, and from the dozens of cars and camper trucks parked in the lot. Bodie is a state park now, and nobody lives here except a couple of rangers.

"This town's had a lot of lives," the young ranger says. "The early mines failed in the '60s, and the Sonora Pass wagon road bypassed the whole area. Then when the Bodie Mine hit in 1876, the place just exploded. There were ten, twelve thousand people living here in the good years.

Ten thousand people, twelve thousand. They used the picks and pans and scales in the museum's glass cases, and read those sallow newspapers filled with long, corny poems. They got their mail in this place; they bought clothes and supplies in that store across the street; they rode in those ironshod buckboards and wagons; ate and slept and made love and died in all those thin, small, canted houses, too dangerous to enter now. The bad men from Bodie. They killed each other in these hollow saloons, and danced on the wooden sidewalks where the tourists tiptoe and take pictures. People talk very quietly in Bodie.

Eleanore Dumont died here — "Madame Moustache," the gambling Frenchwoman from Nevada City. Bodie was the end of the line for her, after twenty-five years of running gambling houses in the gold towns and the railroad camps. She shot herself one summer night, about a mile outside of Bodie.

"Most of the mines were closed by 1883," the ranger says, "but the Bodie and the Standard — that was the first real big one — consolidated, and they kept producing for a long time. Not much, but enough to keep a couple hundred people working here right through the 1930s. It was never really a ghost town, even after the fire."

The great fire of 1932 destroyed most of Bodie, and yet the town hung on for a few years longer. In 1936, the old Roseclip Mine reopened, working over the tailings, the refuse of the old diggings. That lasted into the war years, and then everybody went away.

The young ranger likes Bodie. You can always tell with guides and rangers. There's a sound they get when they're slipping away into the memorized sentences, and they look at a single questioner as though they were talking to a crowd of restless ladies. But this one hasn't yet gotten tired of talking about Bodie and Aurora, and those times.

"It's strange in the winter. I snowshoed in here last winter, and almost all the houses had disappeared. Roofs and chimneys and stovepipes sticking up, galleries sort of balanced on the snow. Boy, that's a strange thing. I got a lot of reading done."

After the red earth bluffs around Bodie (exactly the sort of country where, in the movies, Richard Widmark looks up to see four thousand Indians silently silhouetted on their ponies, licking their warpainted chops as they watch the wagon train pass through the defile), the road winds through a long valley ringed by mountains: grazing land, prettier than the country further south, but drowsy and monotonous on this particular afternoon. Somewhere in the flat stretch between Bridgeport and Coleville, Mike pulls off the road and stops. He points to the right, out over the fading grass to a tiny white tent. "In my experience," he says, "tents like that in the middle of nowhere usually mean little old Basque shepherds. Let's go see."

So we climb through barbed wire and set out across the field, jumping slidy, marshy little streams and kicking up occasional sheep skulls. They are the color and size of peeled boiled potatoes. The tent doesn't seem to get any bigger, but we can see the sheep now. I thought they were gray boulders at first. We walk wide of the tent, so as not to frighten them.

A brown part-collie comes running at us, announcing our arrival: creditably noisy, to be sure, but somehow a bit too shrill and nervous to be really effective. From the tent a voice calls him back. "Niki! *Venga*, Niki!" The dog escorts us the rest of the way to the tent, where a man stands up to meet us. He might easily be fifty years old, by the sun-cracked lines in his face, but his short-cut hair is only gray at the temples, and there is a youngness about his face: a smile that still looks new; an expression at once knowing and vulnerable, as though he had a secret but feared it wasn't a very important one.

He is not Basque, but Spanish, from Navarra in the north. He says he doesn't speak any English, so Mike does almost all the talking. I can follow a good part of the conversation, and Mike fills in the rest. The shepherd won't say exactly how long he's been in the country. "Many years — oh, many years!" He turns his head to the side and breaks up into a spluttering, childlike giggle. The dog comes nearer, reassured, and we can see that he must be almost blind. His eyes are bluish-white, like skim milk.

Inside the tent — which really isn't a bit bigger close to than it seemed from the road — there is a sleeping bag, an ax, a few boxes of canned food and some cooking utensils; a couple of shirts, a lot of bits and scraps of rawhide. He was sewing two large pieces together when we arrived, to make a pouch. Tomorrow he will pack everything on

Sheepherder

104

the donkey grazing with the sheep and lead them up into the mountains, where the pasturing is better now. In the winter he will take them ever higher; and come spring, he will bring them back down here again. This is what he does, alone; this is what he has always done, in Spain and in California. Asked how he likes his life, he shrugs slowly. "There have to be people for everything."

The jets go snaking across the sky, and cars, campers, and mobile homes roll by on the road, most likely on their way to Tahoe. From here, listening to Spanish, looking past the dog and the donkey and the fat gray sprawl of sheep to the big dark house where the *patrona* lives, the road seems as thin and smoky as the jet trails, and as far away. I wonder how many times the shepherd has actually stepped out on that road. Where would he go?

He has a small stack of newspapers in his tent; the man whose sheep he tends subscribes to a Navarra paper for him. It has a lot of international coverage for a regional Spanish newspaper — there are stories on Vietnam, the Congo, *los hippies*, General de Gaulle, the turmoil in China, and the whereabouts of Che Guevara. What does he think of it all, sitting here sewing, journeying back and forth between the mountains and the barbed-wire fence? Something about his presence elicits stupid questions like that, but he goes away into that funny giggle when you ask them.

He likes to talk about Spain, though. "*Siempre pobre*," he says often. "Spain will always be poor." Yet he has heard that the country is growing wealthy these days, that the people are becoming *americanos chiquitos*, little Americans. He will have to go back and see, one day. He mentions *la novia*, a girl back in Navarra, but he is laughing again as he says it. Maybe it's true, and maybe it isn't. I think he's putting us on a little, in a nice, light way.

One odd thing happens. He asks about the book we are writing — will it be about any other states besides California? We say no, and he agrees quickly. No, of course not. You have to have papers, a passport, to cross the state lines.

"That's not true," Mike says. "There is no need of a passport. One can travel freely in this country."

"Anh," the shepherd says. His face flinches and he looks away, making a twitchy motion with one hand. He doesn't believe us; he is genuinely embarrassed for us, to be caught in such a foolish lie. Mike insists, "You don't need a passport to go to another state," but the shepherd won't talk about it any more.

Maybe he heard that in Spain, and never checked it out; more likely, his boss told him, to keep him from looking for better-paying work in Nevada. It would be familiar enough to a European, especially a Spaniard. We say goodby in a very friendly manner, but I think he is a little relieved to see us go.

Mike has a thing about picking out places to retire to and become a chuckling old town character — "loved, but unrespected," as the song says. I'm beginning to do that myself, as we travel. Right now, my first choice would be Alpine County. As I suggested before, I have a natural fondness for places that nobody wants. And I mean it as a compliment when I say that nobody wants Alpine County.

Five hundred people, at most, live here — far less than in any other county of California. The population density, as of 1964, was 0.7 per square mile. Markleeville, the county seat, has one street — and it's a very nice street — and less than a hundred people. (A number of books comment, in hushed tones, that Alpine County committed the California sin of losing population during the war years.) The county has, at this writing, no high school, doctor, hospital, dentist, barber, movie theater, or practicing attorney. I suppose they're overstocked with town characters, but it seems like a fine place. Once the snow falls, it's not even part of California, really.

This was silver land in the old days. Alpine County was pasted together in 1864 from snippets of Amador, Tuolumne, El Dorado, Calaveras, and Mono counties, mainly because of the big strike at Silver Mountain, south of Markleeville. The demonetization of silver in 1873 broke the boom, but mining of several sorts — sulphur, copper, and tungsten, as well as silver — has continued on and off to the present day. There's some lumbering now; some livestock ranching, and a growing tourist trade. Ninety per cent of the county is contained within two national forests, and the hunting and fishing is supposed to be excellent.

But nobody really wants Alpine County! — and in California, that is a great and amazing thing. The governing philosophy of the state, from the very beginning, has been that land exists to be used — mined, plowed, cultivated, leveled, paved, built on, parked on, profited from — that it would be unnatural to leave it alone. Fortunate is the worthless country, and safest to care about. I'm a little worried about a ski resort coming in, as at Mineral King, but you have to take some chances.

The big roads going to Tahoe and Reno bypass Alpine County — which is another good thing — but you can pick up 89 north of Topaz and go over Monitor Pass. Try to make it late enough in the afternoon to get that golden, quiet light slanting from the southwest on the quaking aspens, and the mountain loneliness that comes with that light. Have someone else drive. Sit in the rear seat and look back and down.

It's like that all over. The whole damn county.

Tahoe is an ugly place that exists because of a beautiful place. There's a moral lesson for us all lost in there somewhere. The people who live because Lake Tahoe is beautiful — the resort operators, the motel people, the casino owners, the real-estate dealers, the people who rent waterskis and sell sunglasses, the officials of two states and five counties that border on the lake — all of them know that, ticky-tacky aside, a permanent population of 75,000 (predicted for 1970) will turn the lake into a gray, dim, foul sink, which is unpleasant for waterskiing, depressing to wake up to in your summer cottage, and makes very bad coffee. It's happening already; in the right light you can see the

Desolation Valley

State line, Tahoe

cloudy swirling just below the surface. Everyone is quite concerned, and commissions meet all the time.

But everyone was concerned about Lake Tahoe when I came to California seven years ago, and the blue-ribbon committees were meeting then, and nothing has been done that makes any difference. The California thing has always been to make the money and move on; self-restraint, even in your own commercial interest, is unknown, except at gunpoint. I can understand greed, and accept it as a creative force, but stupidity maddens me more and more as I grow older. Lake Tahoe could be preserved, and the good people could still go on making pots of money, but it isn't going to happen that way. The good people's hearts just aren't in it.

This is what Mark Twain wrote about Lake Tahoe a hundred years ago:

> *So singularly clear was the water, that where it was only twenty or thirty feet deep the bottom was so perfectly distinct that the boat seemed floating in the air! Yes, where it was even eighty feet deep. Every little pebble was distinct, every speckled trout, every hand's-breadth of sand. . . . Down through the transparency of these great depths, the water was not merely transparent, but dazzlingly, brilliantly so. All objects seen through it had a bright, strong vividness, not only of outline but of every minute detail, which they would not have had when seen simply through the same depth of atmosphere. So empty and airy did all spaces seem below us, and so strong was the sense of floating high aloft in mid-nothingness, that we called these boat excursions "balloon voyages."*

Well, there's good hiking and camping to be found in the hills all around the lake; and the lake itself is as shiveringly lovely as Twain ever saw it, when you look down from the hills. But if Sausalito is my place for watching pretty girls, Tahoe is associated forever in my mind with ugly old women: chins like walnuts, cheeks like flapjacks; wandering sullenly in and out of the casinos in the white, bitter daylight.

The whole point is to be camping out. I used to make easy fun of the California idea of roughing it: the endless line of pickup trucks laboring over Tioga Pass or jamming along the Redwood Highway; each with a light motorcycle lashed up front, a fourteen-foot boat trundling behind, and a motel kitchenette stacked in between. Bring the stereo, bring the washer and the Disposall; watch Johnny Carson in the pale Death Valley night. Anyplace I can plug in my hair-dryer is home, in California.

But I've stopped doing that lately. What if they only run the boats in circles; what if they never lie on the ground or bathe in a stream; what if they sit in their pavilions and play gin rummy in the evenings, while their murderous children throw stones at bats and flying squirrels? Me, I sleep on six inches of foam rubber in a VW bus, and when I scramble up a mountain trail far behind Mike, I sound as though I were going to throw a rod. I don't look up very much — there are times when the sudden shock of the sky, after a day of balancing my head between hunched shoulders, makes me dizzy and almost sick. I've backpacked once in my life. I'm entirely for conservation, but I have no true knowledge of the thing I want to conserve. I hate freeways, but I use them once they're there. Who am I to mock at a portable TV? At least, it's bringing in strange stations.

Six in the morning — maybe a quarter to six. No light, but everything clear as an etching, though without depth or color. I appear to be stark naked on a riverbank at five-thirty in the morning, holding a cake of soap. The stones would hurt my feet if I could feel anything. Look at the water tumbling over that snag. It's snow, that's why it looks like that, pearl-gray on the surface, but white as sunlight where the snag rips it open. Oh me. Oh me. My God, it's strong. Hang onto the branch with one hand, wash with the other. *What'll I do with the soap?* Oh me. Ten minutes ago I was sound asleep, and now I'm here. Duck under now, get all the soap off. Five in the morning. Five in the morning.

The middle-aged couple having lunch in their camper, looking at the river out of the open door. Both white-haired, but lean and brown, they might be brother and sister. They have camped all over Europe and Mexico — they've only been back from Austria for a couple of weeks. Now they're going up the Klamath so he can catch a few days of the salmon run before his vacation is over. "I write letters," she says, "and make things my grandchildren don't need."

At Fallen Leaf Lake, near Tahoe, scores of people are lined along the beach, casting into the shallows and hauling in small green-and-silver fish as fast as they can reel. One man, untangling his son's line, explains that the fish were released in the lake last night. "A thousand at a time," he says, "they last about two weeks, maybe three." The little fish don't put up any sort of a fight; they take the hook dutifully and die in the scalding air without flapping. "They don't know where they are," the man says. "I think they go crazy, in a way."

In the morning, eggs are sizzling on all the grills and hibachis, and women line up to wash tin plates in cold water. The children are running around barefoot, exploring people by playing loudly in front of them; but all those Girl Scouts, Campfire Girls, whatever, are still asleep. They were up half the night, singing songs and shooting craps, tying each others' uniforms in knots to get merit badges. Coffeepots burp and chuckle, and the pump splashes; engines turn over; minarets of canvas and nylon come rattling down.

The two very young couples surface slowly in their twisted sleeping bags: the boys shaggy and groaning, the girls hugging their knees through the cloth. They have no tent, so they have to wake in public. None of them are memorably good-looking, and they don't mumble anything of real significance as they get up. They splash their faces, roll up the sleeping bags and strap them on their backs, put their arms around each other, and walk away into the trees.

We are in a small grocery in a very small town near the Oregon border, picking up a box of raisins, the staple food of all our journeys. Lack of raisins necessitates a stop as unarguably as being low on gas, wanting coffee or a San Francisco paper, or having to go. Just ahead of us in the line, a large, fat man with a gambler's mustache over his thick mouth suddenly bursts into speech, as abruptly as though I had just tuned in his station. "Well, you wait a couple of weeks, that's all. You'll see them niggers up here, taking the place over. A couple of weeks, they'll all be up here, all them niggers."

It's savagely hot, this northern August: over a hundred degrees every day for two weeks. You slide around in your own sweat driving the bus. We swim wherever we can, usually in lakes and ponds, but once in the Klamath. It's fairly wide at this point, but shallow — you have to lie flat to have all of your body under water. But it's frighteningly strong; as teasingly irresistible as an adult's strength to a child trying to wrestle. We cling

It's impossible not to root for the Modocs. They were outnumbered 20 to 1, with few weapons and no possibility of reinforcements, and with the measureless weight of Western Civilization coming down on them. They would have been crushed even if the soldiers hadn't cut off their water supply; even if Captain Jack—who must have been a hell of a man—had been able to hold his warring factions together. But they didn't lose what Western Civilization lost.

to rocks, tugging ourselves upstream, waving forlornly to each other when the current breaks our holds and begins to tumble us slowly away toward the rapids. Thirty-pound salmon buck this, and stronger than this, for hundreds of miles. I didn't understand what salmon did until now. A shoulder or a neck out of the water feels as though it were being seared on hot metal. It must be like that for fish, for the salmon and the steelheads. "I still don't know what a steelhead is," Mike says, "but I know it's a magic word. Say *steelhead* to anybody in this country, and they start smiling and talking, even if the beards bother them. *Steelhead* makes everything all right."

In the Cedar Grove campground of Sequoia National Park, we sit under trees in the early evening reading Horatio Hornblower, who is part of the trips, like raisins. We have cheese — half melted in the plastic — and a bottle of wine. A man is looking down at us, saying, "Well, you fellas sure look like you're having a good time. Everything going all right?"

He is fiftyish, not thin, not fat, dressed in clothes that don't register, with one of those stubbly American faces like necks or arms that have begun to develop features. He has a bus like Renata, but much newer, a camper. "I've got five women traveling with me," he says. "Wife, two daughters, my wife's sister, and her daughter. It's real comfortable, but it's sure got the camper smelling like powder and lipstick. I saw you two fellas, just thought I'd see how you were getting along."

The talk is mostly about the buses, comparing horsepower, mileage, oil consumption. It's another exchange of magic words, like *steelhead*. We offer him some wine, but he shakes his head. "No, thank you, better not. I was just on my way to wash up for dinner, but you fellas just looked so content, I thought I'd say hello. You have a good time now."

Cars. Somewhere around Alturas (high prairie, sandy gold and sandy white; very like the Midwest, except for transparent Shasta projected on the sky), we pass slowly through one town or another, not stopping. A long car, now painted with sunset swirls and abstract-expressionist *graffiti*, but unmistakably a hearse, is stalled in the middle of the road, and four boys are peering under the hood. They might be a rock band, from their dress and their white young faces, like the faces of Orthodox Jewish children. They look terribly stranded in the empty street: lonely and somehow endangered, and I have a feeling that we should probably stop and help them. But we are looking for a milk-shake place; and these moments come and go so fast that by the time you make up your mind there's no place to turn around, anyway. We do come back through the town again, still checking for milk shakes, but the prismal hearse is gone.

Wandering around the Lava Beds National Monument (a good, lonesome, windy place where some 60 Modoc Indians once held off more than 1200 soldiers for half a year, to keep from being resettled in the country of their Klamath enemies), we run into three spelunkers — cave explorers. They are college kids who spend their summers mapping caves for the Geodetic Survey. Their bus looks somewhat like a remodeled paddy-wagon: they have hammocks slung in the back, and there is a clutter of rock-climbing equipment — ropes, pitons, hammers, lanterns. This will be Walt's first descent since he got smashed up last Christmas in a cave in Nevada. It took them about ten hours to get him out, because he couldn't move, and they couldn't reach him.

Supper on the baseball field at Ferndale. Ferndale is an utterly beautiful, utterly ridiculous town just south of Eureka, in the black-earth dairy country of the Eel River Bottom. I don't want to describe it thoroughly, because the best way to go there is to go without expectations, to be on your way somewhere else, and have to stop. It's a Victorian town, with the kind of voluptuous, birthday-cake architecture they call "carpenter-Gothic" — all scrolls, filigree, inlays, helices, and those fish scales you see on old North Coast houses. The buildings have been repainted and restored in the last five years, and Ferndale is gradually becoming an art colony, with some of that Carmel quaintness creep-

Ferndale

ing into the windows and the storefronts. Even so, there's a leanness, a sharp New England spine under all the frosting; the town is still whole, one piece of time, though now it knows it is.

That first evening, the feeling was like having stepped into one of those first-grade readers about Jim and Judy: the white, clean, milkman town where Dr. Brown comes to the house and there's a baby; where everyone is what he's named — Father, Mother, Grandpa, Mr. Grocer, Mr. Butcher — and where no one is unhappy, or poor, or ever unsafe. On Gunhill Road, we knew that our lives weren't like that, but we never questioned the reality of that world, or its meaning. I still recognize it immediately, though it never existed.

The two teams are warming up as Mike slices salami, breaks eggs into the pan, cuts up onions, experiments with cheese and canned chili. It's a cool, cloudless sunset: a wash of green, a thin crimson rim. Cars come driving in as it darkens, parking all around the outfield; the kind of fat cars they have in the Jim-and-Judy books. They leave their lights on with their engines running, since the field hasn't any floodlights. Even the police car is there, with two young, nailbiting cops who look as though they might have been playing ball here last summer. The players run and swing and slide in the headlights; and one large, dirty dog, chased off after each play, keeps locating its master during the next one, and running to him.

Mother Lode

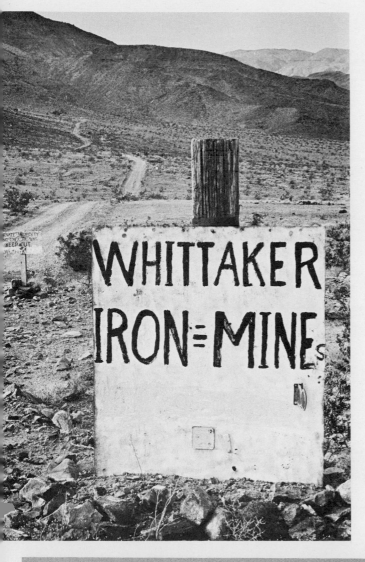

Hornitos Graveyard

Near Death Valley

Tombstone, Knights Ferry

Stage coach for tourists near Columbia

I don't mourn the old houses that this freeway sliced out of Nevada City simply because they were old. A town should have what it needs, whatever relic may be the price. But Nevada City didn't need a freeway.

Sutterville Main Street

Old store wall, Hornitos

Morning mist, Mother Lode County

Mariposa Court House

CHEVRON DEALER

EMERGENCY AAA ROAD SERVICE

I.O.O.F.

MAREMONT

MUFFLERS INSTALLED

Car·Care SPECIALIST

TUNE UP

LUBRICATION

COMPLETE

FAST EXPERT

WHEEL ALINEMENT HERE

FREE CHECK UP

8. A Wild Time for a Few Years

(GOLD RUSH COUNTRY)

The Gold Rush country lies due east of Tahoe, in the Sierra foothills. Route 49, the Mother Lode Hideway, running from Mariposa to Sierra City, covers the extent of the area pretty well. It can't include the far northwestern outposts like Weaverville and Whiskeytown; but it does take in the "Northern Diggins," the camps north of Georgetown, where the Mother Lode is generally considered to end. Towns like Bodie and Aurora, on the eastern side of the Sierras, belong to another era, after the Fraser River rush and the Washoe stampede of 1859. The Mother Lode rush had been over for four or five years by then.

That's the amazing thing about it, in the end. It lasted so incredibly short a time — California gold production was already declining in 1853 — and it changed the country so completely and finally. The present-day New Yorker's dream of gracious, easy, empty California is an image of a Mexican province in the decade or so before James Marshall got to poking around in his employer's millrace. The days of the great land grants and the great families — Vallejo, Alvarado, Peralta, Carrillo, Castro — when there was room enough and time enough for everybody to be comfortable and courteous, except Indians. The fur trappers came and went; and there were people crossing the mountains even then — barefoot, sick, starving, burning with that eastern dream of magic. There was room enough. It was the time of the amiable kings. One of the kings was named John Sutter.

> *He was soaked to the skin and dripping water. Very much excited . . . He drew a*
> *rag from his pocket. Opening it carefully, he held it before me in his hand . . .*
> *John A. Sutter:* New Helvetia Diary

The gold ruined Sutter. Thousands of emigrants overran his fort, his city-state on the banks of the Sacramento, and spread through his land like bollweevils; paying no rent, cutting his timber, running off his Indian workers, and helping themselves to the cattle his *vaqueros* had abandoned to go to the mines. He retreated helplessly before the new men, and so did most of the northern lords. There was nothing to be done. Reading the accounts of those days, you get the feeling that most people understood that something irrevocable had happened: that time had trembled and their world had fallen down. California has always been subject to timequakes.

South of Monterey, the old days endured a while longer, until the end of the Civil War.

Mokelumne Hill. If there is one original building remaining of a gold town, the odds are 7–2
that it will be an Odd Fellows hall. Wells Fargo offices come in a poor second, and banks third.

The Gold Rush's immediate effect on the south was to create an enormous market for beef cattle. It was a wild time for a few years, but when the boom collapsed, the old pastoral economy broke with it, and that was really the end. After California became a state, the Land Act of 1851 drove many of the *rancheros* into bankruptcy attempting to validate their titles; and floods, drought, locusts, and disease finished off the rest. By 1869, when the Union Pacific Railroad was completed, the land had passed from the kings.

It was all coming, of course. Settlement, statehood, the railroad; the rancheros' decline, and the development of a varied grain and fruit agriculture; the growth of cities and supercities in a series of great hiccups — it would all have happened sooner or later, and not too differently, even without the gold. But the Gold Rush speeded everything up. The Gold Rush set California off on that unique, terrifying pace that telescopes generations and uses up whole decades in a couple of years. It is this pace that makes people assume that California has no history, not as Massachusetts and Virginia have histories.

Actually, California has more history than all the other states, because its nature since 1849 has been to keep turning the present into real, dead, museum history, as neatly and implacably as it churns pine trees into plywood. It's like the disc jockey who shouts in the car, "Oldies but goodies, folks! — here's one from back in 1966! Who remembers . . . ?" You can stand still and feel the present tearing past, pulling out from under your feet, like the beach sand when a wave is sliding back into the sea: digging your grave. That's that California feeling.

The foothill zone is scooter country. The phrase is a personal one, and hard to translate. Generally, the kind of land that I think of as being made for motorscooter traveling is not magnificent, but small-scaled enough so that it doesn't seem completely ridiculous and lonely to be pooting around on the surface of it. (Huge loneliness is all right too, sometimes.) Proper scooter country tends to be hilly, partly because it makes the driving more interesting — and slows most Lambrettas and Vespas down enough to give you time to pay attention to things — and partly because things fold closer to you: colors and smells, branches overhead, the brittle old roads. Smells are very important. Smells may be the best thing about driving scooters.

The foothills smell like apples. In the spring they are colored as though a very young child had painted them, splashing lupine and adder's tongues, meadowfoam and mountain lilac all over the place, with no pattern except pleasure; now and then spilling the bottle of greenish-black chaparral. Autumn is drawn by an older hand, less self-indulgent, aware of things like line and light and composition. In autumn the oaks explode, and the shaggy, dusty, undignified digger pines turn almost blue; but the maples and the dogwoods are as delicate as though they were made of bits of glass or hammered metal. You half expect to hear the leaves chime softly together when the wind blows through them.

New England. I suppose because New England was all of the world that wasn't New York to me for so much of my childhood, I'm liable to recognize it in almost any reasonably bright and bumpy country. In the main, the Gold Rush camps don't look very much like Vermont towns, except for the places like Auburn, Grass Valley, and Weaverville that grew on into tidy cities around the tiny old grain of shacks and pit shafts and saloons. But the feeling that comes to me here, just poking around, is the feeling of being eight and nine and ten, poking around the white wooden houses, and the dark stores that smelled of root beer and sold strange brands of candy. I've even rediscovered some of the nice, corny books that I read only in those summers, and never found again.

The old towns are all alike in certain obvious ways. The image that comes first to mind is of the beautiful, heavy iron shutters on the stores and the banks. Most of the buildings are of wood, with the usual exceptions like jails and mills and express offices, and occasional odd ones like Columbia, which is built almost entirely of red brick. A stone-and-adobe mixture is common, especially in the southern mines, but it doesn't affect the thin, broken feeling of things. The houses are hardly ever more than two stories high. Some

General Store, Lotus

have galleries fringing the second floor, supported from underneath by posts; but the dominant feature of gold-town architecture is the false front — the high, blind façade, often elaborately eaved and corniced, but as uncompromisingly rectangular as Puritan stock could rule them. Sighting down a row of them makes me laugh and shiver at the same time.

There's something rather grand and sad about the false fronts, after you stop remembering them from movies and start to see them. The small, severe buildings that they hide have withered and fallen in like grapes, but the fronts themselves hold up surprisingly well. Many are still as straight and sharp-cornered as windowpanes. The timbers have warped and sprung as much as they will — now the house will have to collapse completely before the façade goes down. It is as though all the responsibility for supporting the ruin behind it had been laid on the false front, and somehow made it real.

The relics of the camps are less interesting in themselves than they are as touchstones: points at which the imagination can sometimes make a moment's contact with the way it was. In Coloma, where the sawmill that James Marshall was building for John Sutter has just been reconstructed, as far along as Marshall ever got, I find myself staring at an ancient jail cell: an iron box, somewhat smaller than a privy, standing on end, naked, near the picnic tables. People always come up to try their hands on the iron slats. In Mariposa, where lode mining began, I look at dozens of chunks of gold-bearing quartz; in Hornitos, it's the Mexican graves, the little adobe mounds that looked like bake ovens. A covered bridge leading into Knight's Ferry; a stagecoach stop that has become a garage; leather hinges on the door of a cabin near Jackson. Square nails, bits of harness, bullets and spoons and hand-made barbed wire in the class cases, together with all kinds of tools made for tasks that don't exist anymore. Locust trees mark the passage of the Chinese far more faithfully than the graveyards do.

The different methods of getting the gold out left different marks on the land. Placering — the classic process of straining a whole creek through a rocking sieve — brought the towns, and lode mining created the scores of overgrown shafts and tunnels; crumbled shut now, many of them. The scars have not all grown over yet, where the hydraulic nozzles blasted into the hills. They would have torn the foothills apart and washed them down the Sacramento, if hydraulicking hadn't been outlawed in 1893. The dredges came next. Up at Jackson Gate, two 68-foot wheels bearing 176 buckets apiece were turning at the Kennedy Mine until 1942. The roadsides of this country are drifted with millions of tons of tailings dumped by the dredges.

Some of the great floating beasts got stranded in their own tailings and were abandoned; others were trapped when the new lakes they cut dried up around them. Just south of Oroville, there's a dredge caught in a cracked, thick place that now happens to belong to a motel. It looks very strange in the motel light of an autumn evening: cold and lost, out of time. You could stage *Showboat* on it.

(The watchman gets forlornly hysterical when he sees someone taking pictures of the dredge. Mike, who has been here before, says that there's a lot less of it than there was last time. Someone may be stripping it illegally and selling the pieces for scrap.)

The cemeteries, by the way, are good places in which to learn about the early days. Looking at the dates on the stones, you realize that California settlers in the nineteenth century didn't live a lot longer than the average Elizabethan. They died in their forties and fifties, of drowning, the plague, pneumonia, cave-ins, fights, and maybe just of being worn down faster, like lead pencils. There was a hell of a lot of infant mortality; it's quite common to find a family plot where only one out of five or six children lived into adolescence. Even when you can't read the stones, you can tell the children's graves by the standard bas-relief lambs. After a while, the dusty, muffled impact starts to reach you.

The different kinds of names are off in bunches, as they always are. Larsens lie down with Hansens, Phelans with Ryans, Ortegas with Martinezes, Schlegels with Zinssers, Willstatters, and Mullers — there are a surprising amount of German names. No Chinese. The only people who seem to be sown more or less at random are the Indians: the small, split, rotted boards, stuck nameless into the ground, turn up freely in every section, like a kind of dark weed peculiar to old cemeteries. No lambs on these.

Except for the Indians, the headstones have one thing in common: almost all of them mention that the person who is buried here was born somewhere else. But they usually say "native," and it makes a difference. *Native of Kentucky. Native of Maine. Native of County Antrim, Ireland. Native of France.* It's that particular lonely word that haunts me. *Native of Kirkcudbrightshire, Scotland, drowned in the Stanislaus River April 4, 1858.*

Well, they pulled their wagons up cliffs to get here, piece by piece — the ones who didn't sail around the Horn, or walk across Mexico or the Isthmus. When the trails got too steep, they emptied the wagons and took them apart, and lugged everything as far as they had to. I saw a photograph in some museum: chest and sacks and timbers all over the road; men stretching to hand things on up to other men; the women taking this chance to re-pack bags and boxes; and the mountains so hard and real, even in that dim old picture, that they make the people look comic, like high school actors staging a pageant.

Columbia is easily the best-preserved of the gold towns, because of its brick construction. Even the dirt streets have a powdery red tinge, while the countryside around it is curiously pale and bare — literally washed out. Columbia was the greatest of the southern mines. More than twenty thousand people lived here once, and they sluiced and tunneled the red soil for something like ninety million dollars in gold between 1850 and 1940; though the bulk of that was taken within the first twenty years. Joseph Henry Jackson reports a legend that St. Anne's Church stands on the only unworked land for miles around. It must have had a close call in the 1870s, when the miners were starting to take the town apart to get at the dirt beneath.

Columbia has been a historic state park since 1945, which is another reason for its excellent condition, and it must surely be the biggest tourist attraction in the Mother Lode country. It's not alive as Auburn and Nevada City are alive, but it does feel like a real town where people live. Disneyland doesn't have that. Columbia is quite aware of that atmosphere — and thereby hangs a funny story.

Some years ago, it was suggested that the citizens of Columbia should all wear Gold Rush clothes during their working hours. Merchants and businessmen might dress in frock coats, vests, and beaver hats; women would have on the high-necked, long-waisted calico dresses; and miners, stage drivers, and bartenders could wear the proper costumes of their professions. Everyone agreed, except a local artist named Charles Surendorf.

At this point, I would like to observe that California produces art galleries at the remorseless rate with which India produces Indians. There must be an established statistic: every fifty-four seconds, somebody looks thoughtfully at an old barn or an abandoned sweatshop, and says, "Now, wouldn't this be a marvelous place for an art gallery!" I'm not sure about Southern California, but I know that in the north, being a ghost town is no insurance against having a gallery. They multiply where bars and antique shoppes go under; they thrive in wastelands where even the real-estate dealers give up. People love the idea of running an art gallery. I think that every so often some sociologist should make a survey of the current American images of a satisfying life. I'm sure it would be an important and useless thing to know.

Anyway, Surendorf said no. He said he'd wear funny clothes when he felt like wearing funny clothes. Push came rapidly to shove, and Surendorf had to give up his own gallery in the town. He sells his paintings out of his home now, and seems to be doing very well. He is also writing a novel, based on the legend of a drunken miner who called down the curse of the gods upon Columbia.

Mike and I each bought the same print from him: a dark, powerful drawing, full of grotesque motion, showing three men dragging a fourth toward his unseen death. It's the ghastly Barclay lynching, which happened here in 1855. They forgot to tie Barclay's hands, and he grabbed onto the rope and wouldn't let go, though everyone begged him to be a good sport; so they had to break his hands with pistol butts.

It's a warm day, and the wide main street is crowded with tourists. The children are scrambling into the stagecoach, which has just pulled up in front of the Stage Drivers' Rest — it makes a regular circuit of the town — or tugging their parents off to go placering in the stream. "We can keep the gold, Pop, they let you keep anything you find!" The people eat ice cream under the ailanthus trees, looking up at deep windows behind gilded wrought-iron balconies. They wander in and out of the firehouse, the saloons, the hotel; they peer at gold scales and account books in the Wells Fargo office. In the barbershop, the barber sits on a stool, trying to pick out *Margie* on the mandolin. He wears a handlebar mustache and muttonchop whiskers; full-sleeved white shirt, gay vest, arm garters. A placard on the wall reminds you that this is a working barbershop, and the prices are the lowest I've ever seen in California. I wonder if anyone ever does come in for a haircut.

It's touristy in spots, but Mike points out that the gold towns were always gaudy and

Charles Surendorf, artist, in Columbia

touristy. Good taste and the beginning of death usually arrive together. "There's only so much you can do," he says. "You can knock everything down and blast a freeway through — just grind it up and pave it all over, the way they're doing in Nevada City. You can leave the whole place to rot, like Hornitos, or crap it up with little souvenir shoppes, like in Sonora. If you're Lucius Beebe, you can buy Virginia City and play with it for a while. I think Columbia is about as good a compromise as I've seen."

"I like places that work, I guess. The barbershop, or the courthouse in Mariposa. It's a museum, and people come walking through all the time, taking pictures, but it's the courthouse too. I like that, continuity."

"Restoration's a funny business," Mike says. "I was in England when they were fixing up Hadrian's Wall. They were being so careful not to improve anything — almost to think second-century Roman thoughts while they worked on the wall. It was a beautiful job, but I used to wonder what the people in those little Northumberland towns made of it, and what they said to each other."

127

St. George Hotel, Mother Lode County

"Hell, no," the lady says. She runs the St. George Hotel in Volcano. "People live here," she says, "people are building all the time. You can't call Volcano a ghost town, like the others."

The photographs in the bar show Volcano as it looked in 1915, 1876; in 1862, when the hotel first opened. Volcano was already withering then: hydraulic mining had begun, and the town was being slowly washed away in mud. But a few years earlier, there were five thousand people in Volcano, and they built with stone. The surface gravel was incredibly rich — you very nearly did kick up gold walking in the street, as my father believed of America when he was a boy. They had a Thespian Society in Volcano, and a Miners' Library Association.

"I live here because I like it," she says. "I wasn't washed up in Volcano. I've lived all over California, and I chose this place. Too many folks moving in would ruin it. We like it the way it is, just quiet and friendly and unexciting. But it's not a damn bit dead."

Across the road there is a stone wall with four shuttered doors in it, and a creeper-grown pit beyond the doors. More than ninety million dollars came out of this town.

The party in the next room got drunk early, and everyone went off to bed. She carries glasses and bottles back into the bar, and then sits talking softly with the bartender. "I thought she was going to cry, but she didn't. She was holding it in all the time, though, after that."

The bartender is fixing them both drinks, without asking what she wants. "Yeah, well, he's a mean old devil, but she's just a fool. I told you what happened when they were in here Tuesday, when you went to Jackson. She's just a damn fool."

"I liked the girl who came in with Dennis. That was her playing the piano."

Their voices grow quieter, and they themselves seem to be moving steadily away, drifting on the long brown-and-gold river of the bar. "No, I don't think he meant to say that. I'll tell you what I *think* he meant — "

"Sure, he meant it. Listen, I've watched him for a long time now."

Sierraville at five-thirty on an autumn afternoon. This is another of Mike's towns to be old in. We're always coming through Sierraville late in the day. I've never seen the sunlight falling straight on the tawny grass, or on the old hotel across the street; rounded at the corners, like a worn cake of soap. Sierraville was never a gold town, but a crossroads. Four stagecoach lines used to meet here, where we get gas and I call home. I think the false-front next to the gas station might have been the place.

It's cold, and the shadows make the street seem wider and deeper than it is. You can see the air — tea-rose color — but not be in it, as though you were looking into water through a glass. Three boys in their early teens are out in the street, running around, shoving each other, laughing and cursing. Adults call it all play, but it isn't really. I remember.

Two of the boys are bugging the third one, who is tall and skinny and wears his hair shoulder-length. They call him Weirdy. "Over here, Weird! Hey — hey, Weirdy!" He must be the only kid in Sierraville with long hair.

"Spirit screens" in the Weaverville Joss House. The traditional Taoist belief is that evil spirits can travel only in a straight line, and not around corners.

Last worshiper at Weaverville Joss House, Mr. Moon Lee

I think I like Weaverville best. It's nowhere near the Mother Lode, but away up in Trinity County, on the edge of the Salmon-Trinity Wilderness, which is handsome, glacier-cut land — quite a lot like Alpine County, but with a more active Chamber of Commerce. Weaverville was one of the original Gold Rush towns, and has been the county seat since 1850. The mines here played out later than in other places (the hydraulic workings at La Grange, four miles northwest, were producing through World War I), and by the time the gold was gone, Weaverville had become a real city of brick and iron and adobe; never to be wealthy or notorious again, but always alive. It's a quiet town, with a nice dignity. There isn't much work to be had locally, and people live mostly off lumbering, tourism, and a little dairy farming. The winters are hard. James Hilton called Weaverville a true Shangri-La, and I like it fine myself, but the kids probably can't wait to get out.

Weaverville was a wide-open heller in the beginning, though. Joseph Henry Jackson tells a story about a Shangri-La called Spanish Corral, on the outskirts of town, which, for one reason and another, was finally commanded by the law to close its door," — the front one. It was obediently nailed shut. Nothing was said about the back door, through which staff and customers continued to come and go." That's a fine story.

The story of the Bridge Gulch Massacre comes from here too. In 1852, a Weaverville man named Anderson was killed by Wentoon Indians. A party of miners tracked the Indians to their camp at a natural bridge near Hayfork, and there slaughtered 153 of them — about one third women and children. Two small girls survived, and were raised by white families in Weaverville.

During the gold years, there were several thousand Chinese in Trinity County, and Weaverville's colony numbered about two thousand. The Chinese who lived here fared much better than most Chinese in California, in spite of — more likely, because of — the fact that they paid a special tax of four dollars per month per miner. They opened stores and restaurants, took over gambling houses, and built a Taoist temple, a joss house. But they never seem to have thought of themselves as settlers, or as anything but exiles. They were always going to go home.

It's ironic enough that Weaverville's most celebrated exhibit today is its old joss house (not the original — that burned down in 1873, and the present temple was built in the following year); but it's curiouser still to reflect that the temple has been preserved only because Moon Lee's family weren't very good miners. Taoists do say that the universe knows exactly what it's doing.

Moon Lee has a good face. He runs a hardware store on the main street, a little way down from the two famous spiral staircases of Weaverville: graceful and mysterious as dancers; the last of seven such, according to one story. The cloudy photograph on Moon Lee's business card shows two young boys sitting in a gaunt, slatty cart drawn by an even slattier horse. Above the boy's heads run the words, SERVING THE PUBLIC SINCE 1909.

"My family, we just didn't make it," Moon Lee says, smiling. "In 1906, there was a big fire in Chinatown, and everybody started to move away. They went back to China, some of them went to San Francisco, Stockton. We couldn't go anywhere. We went broke in the mines, so we had to stay here. A few others had to stay too, but most people went away."

He touches the smaller of the two boys in the old picture. "That's me. Me and my brother. We did a little truck gardening, my family, and we sold things off that wagon. I was seven, eight years old. We were so poor, today I don't know how we lived. There was a lady who had a farm, and she let us live there. If not for her, I don't know. We were supposed to pay her thirty dollars a month, but most times we couldn't pay it. She let us stay anyway."

The turn began when one of the Lee girls married a man who paid a surprisingly large bride-price to her parents. Then the brother who drove the cart with Moon Lee died, and a small insurance policy enabled the Lees to buy the farm they had been living on. All the others left Weaverville in time, but Moon Lee has always been here.

But about the joss house. Moon Lee and his wife Dorothy are the only Chinese in Weaverville now. Their children are grown and gone, and none of them today believe in their ancestors' religion: in Taoism's spirit screens and fortune sticks, its votive food offerings, and its supple cosmology of gods and demons. "It's all right," Moon Lee says. "They learned different from me, and they came to believe different ways. But I have worshiped in this one place all my life, you know. My grandfather helped to build it. But when I die and my wife dies, there won't be anybody. Nobody would take care of the temple. So I gave the temple to the state, to be a museum. That way, somebody will always be there, looking after it."

Deeding the temple to the state of California turned out to be a tricky procedure. Legally, the joss house wasn't Moon Lee's to give away; it had belonged to a large syndicate of Chinese families, all long vanished from Weaverville. His own title had first to be established before the temple could be signed over and accepted. It was dedicated as a state historical monument on July 4, 1961. Moon and Dorothy Lee are permitted to worship there as long as they live.

It's strange. Moon Lee is an American who has lived the classic American story, and come out of it with a good face. He has been broke and hungry, and now he is a comfortable, respected citizen, and an influential one. Recently he was appointed to the California Highway Commission: he is the first Chinese ever to be a member of the seven-man group, but it seems more important to him that he is the only member from northern California in many years. When Mike asks him jokingly if he plans to get a lot of big new roads pushed through Trinity County, he replies seriously, "No, I couldn't do that. I have to think about the whole state." He is so proud of being on the California Highway Commission that it begins to seem something to be proud of.

But until he dies, Moon Lee will cross the moon bridge to the joss house, to burn incense before a 3000-year-old altar; to leave food on a little table and wine in a stone urn; and to kneel to gods of gold and bronze and teakwood, addressing to them prayers at

Weaverville stairs

least as old as they are. He has seen to it that they will be preserved when he is gone, but no one else will ever pray to them. I hope the gods answer him — the last Chinese in Weaverville — while they have the chance to do anything for anyone.

Another Weaverville story, probably the most famous and confused one. On July 14, 1854, a battle was fought between two factions of local Chinese at a ravine called Five-Cent Gulch, a mile east of town. That much is generally accepted, and so is the fact that one group defeated the other. What isn't at all clear is the number of casualties — estimates range from two to fourteen, with deaths varying accordingly — and the cause of the trouble is as obscure today as it was then. White eyewitnesses wrote up accounts and conjectures, but the Chinese never said anything.

Sutterville scene

A few of the pikes and tridents and straw shields that were made for the combatants by kindly local artisans are on exhibit in the joss house museum today. The guide plays down the story of the "China War," but his own theory about it sounds more probable than most. "What I think," he says, "is that a few white men maybe started whipping up the Chinese against each other. Just for fun, you know. Family feuds, tongs, people from different parts of China — it wouldn't have been too hard. But the way I've heard it, there wasn't a real battle. The Chinese caught on pretty fast that they'd been had, and the only man who actually got killed was a white man. Now I'm not sure, but apparently he was one of the men who'd been going around among the Chinese, egging them on to fight. Of course, nobody's really certain."

When I repeat the story to Mike, he smiles slowly; as beatifically as one can smile without actually being beatified. "That's nice," he says. "That's excellent. Every once in a while."

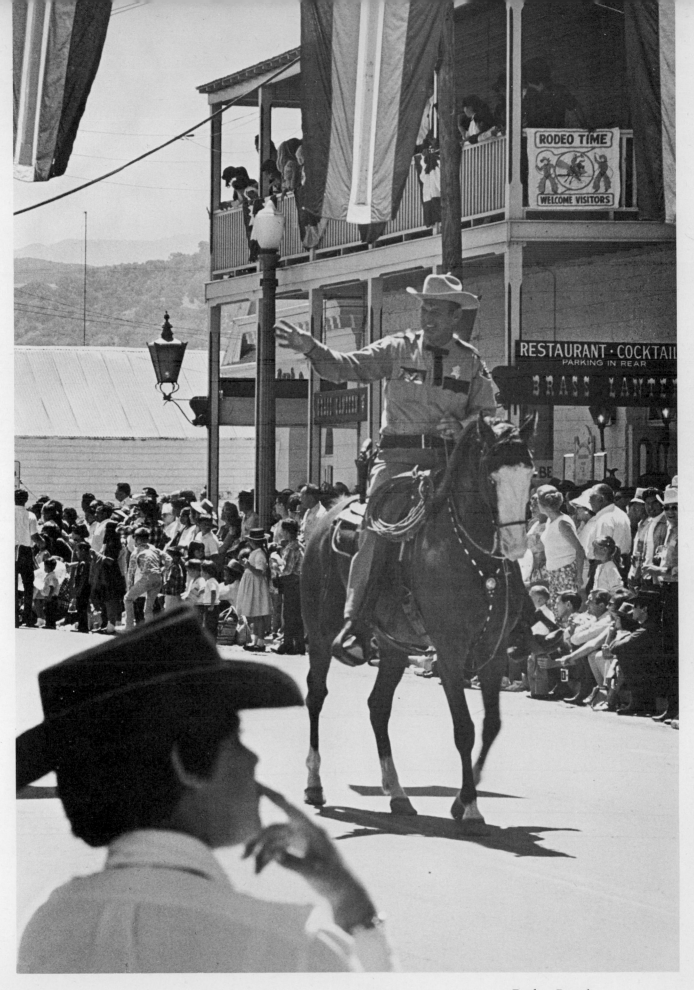

Rodeo Parade

Jackass Hill is about ten miles west of Sonora, just beyond Tuttletown. Mark Twain referred to it as Jackass Gulch when he wrote about the three months he spent there in the winter of 1864–65, as the guest of Jim and Bill Gillis and Dick Stoker. The Gillis cabin burned down long ago, but it has been restored and made a state monument because Mark Twain lived there for a little while. There is a sober-faced foolishness about this — it would have been seemlier to preserve the cabin as a monument to Jim Gillis, who made up the bluejay yarn, as well as a few others that Twain retold in *Huckleberry Finn* and *Roughing It* — but I never thought of not visiting Jackass Hill. Like Robert Paul Smith, I discovered at an early age that Mark Twain was God; and there's probably nothing to see on Mount Sinai, either. You just go and stand there, and sign the guest book.

One fine irony that Twain would surely have appreciated — although he did tend to grow divinely wrathful on the subject in later years — is the way that his name continues to be linked here with that of Bret Harte. There is a town called TwainHarte northeast of Sonora, and the two names are all over the motels, gas stations, diners, and shopping centers. Harte was a phony, and Mark Twain was a genius; but between the two of them, they probably spent about half a year in the Mother Lode region. Harte actually stayed a couple of nights at Jackass Hill, ten years before Twain arrived; he borrowed twenty dollars from Jim Gillis, and passed on to his brief but flaring glory as the bard and chronicler of an imaginary land called California. But Twain's California wasn't real either — yet his lies are true, and Harte's aren't. That's the great advantage of being God.

Jackass Hill had been a coarse-gold boom town in the early fifties, but it was long over there in 1865, except for the people like the Gillises still hunting out pocket mines. Twain had come to California from the wild new days of the Comstock Lode, and he found the foothills sad and ghostly. There's a famous passage in *Roughing It* about the vanished towns that had once boiled with "labor, laughter, music, dancing, swearing, fighting, shooting, stabbing — a bloody inquest and a man for breakfast every morning — *everything* that delights and adorns existence. . . ." But he was making it up — Harte could have done as well, and often did. He is most genuine and moving when he talks about the "grassy dead solitude" of Jackass Hill, and the people who lived there."

> *. . . The mere handful of miners still remaining had seen the town spring up, spread, grow, and flourish in its pride; and they had seen it sicken and die, and pass away like a dream. With it their hopes had died, and their zest of life. . . . One of my associates in the locality, for two or three months, was a man who had had a university education; but now for eighteen years he had decayed there by inches, a bearded, rough-clad, clay-stained miner, and at times, among his sighings and soliloquizings, he unconsciously interjected vaguely remembered Latin and Greek sentences — dead and musty tongues, meet vehicles for the thoughts of one whose dreams were all of the past, whose life was a failure; a tired man, burdened with the present and indifferent to the future; a man without ties, hopes, interests, waiting for rest and the end.*

Bigfoot and McClarin

At the junction of Highways 299 and 96, in the town of Willow Creek, west of Weaverville, a young man named Walter James McClarin is carving a Bigfoot out of a redwood stump. The Bigfoot is — presumably — a legend peculiar to the northwestern counties: a great, shaggy, manlike creature of the back country, kin to fabulous beasts like the Hidebehind, the Hoopsnake, the Bammat, and the one-winged birds that fly round and round a mountain peak all their lives. But Jim McClarin believes in the Bigfoot, and he is making a statue of one. It has taken him most of the summer.

He is working on the statue in the easy orange light of an August evening; standing on a platform, for the stump is fourteen feet tall. The rough shaping was done with an ax, but at this stage he is chipping at the head with a couple of small chisels. His Bigfoot looks more like a gorilla than anything, with its long-armed body balanced on legs that don't seem made to support it erect; with its long upper lip, and the small, deep-set eyes under heavy brows. "That's not the supraorbital ridge, though," Jim says, "it's meant to be hair. The Bigfoot's forehead isn't at all like an ape's."

Klamath River

Two boys and two girls, all in their teens, are watching him work. I had half-expected to find him surrounded by hecklers, but these kids are being very polite and respectful. It's a funny scene: the boys with their shirts off, tan and blank, but pleasant; the girls looking pretty and dissatisfied; and Jim McClarin stepping back and forth above them, answering their questions in a soft voice that can hardly be heard over the highway traffic. He has a beard, and he wears his hair fairly long, with a headband. He has a nice, plain face, with a quick smile and very bright blue eyes.

"No, I don't think there are many of them," he says in answer to one of the boys. "In this country they're probably spread thin through the Pacific Northwest. There's so little wild country left for them to hide in, and there's less all the time. I think they're bound to be discovered very soon."

The other boy asks, "What're you gonna do if you find one? You gonna shoot it?"

Even the plump, sullen little chick in the muu-muu knows it's a dumb question. She snorts and sighs, but Jim replies amiably, "With a camera. I'd try to make it understand that I was friendly, but the thing I'd like most right now is to get a really clear picture of a Bigfoot. Then I could work to have them put under federal protection, so nobody could shoot them. That's what I want."

He urges them to read a book called *On the Trail of the Abominable Snowman*, by Ivan T. Sanderson. It was this book that first interested him in the legend of the *yeti* when he came across it at Humboldt State College, where he is a fourth-year zoology major.

When they leave, the boys say, "Thank you for talking to us, thanks very much." And the girl in the muu-muu assures him, "If I saw one, I wouldn't kill it."

Over dinner he talks about the Bigfoot quite freely, showing none of the grim gleam of the Nut. He feels like a sensible, humorous guy who happens to be convinced that a gigantic relative of man — cousin, half-brother, or even closer — inhabits the forests of Humboldt County, as well as the high slopes of the Himalayas; and perhaps the green African dark, where there has long been talk of something that is neither a gorilla nor a chimpanzee, but very big. He collects stories of Bigfoot sightings and encounters, sifting them for veracity as best he can. The most memorable of the tales is this one:

"The man told me that he was sleeping in his car on a country road. He was awakened by something shaking the car — he thought it was an earthquake at first. But it stopped, and then it started again, and he saw the creature that was doing it. It was huge, and it stank. That's one thing all the Bigfoot stories have in common, the terrible smell. It was rocking the car and beating on it, and when he shouted to scare it away, it didn't scare. Then he leaned on the horn, and the thing turned and ran away down the road. He says it ran on two legs, like a man."

Jim believes the story — though the unprovoked aggressiveness of the Bigfoot is unusual — but he is skeptical about others, such as the account of the man who claims to have been captured by a family of *yetis*. "They didn't harm him, he says, but kept him penned up in a canyon, apparently as a sort of pet for the little ones. He escaped by getting the male to try some of his snuff — they were very curious about things like that — and while it was coughing and choking and running for water, he got away." Jim adds that he doesn't consider this man a truly reliable source. He drinks a lot. And yet, some of the details do fit the image of the Bigfoot that he is gradually forming in the same careful way that he shapes the redwood statue.

"There are just too many similar accounts for the whole thing to be a hoax. I've studied all the reports I could get hold of, and certain things keep recurring. The *yeti* stand between seven and eight feet tall, and must weigh over four hundred pounds, judging by the depth of the tracks that have been found. Some of the footprints may be fakes, but I'm pretty sure about a few of them. *Yetis* live in family groups; they walk erect, and have an opposable thumb. They smell bad — to us — and they're covered with thick hair, which ranges through about the same shades as our hair. When they're angry or frightened, they scream like metal tearing. They make nests of branches to sleep in, like gorillas. Generally they're remarkably shy and inoffensive; but a man in one of Theodore Roosevelt's hunting

parties was killed, bitten to death, by what I think was a Bigfoot. There are a couple of other cases too. But you usually find that the *yeti* had been attacked first, or thought it had."

It has taken Jim most of the summer to carve the Bigfoot. The Chamber of Commerce donated the redwood stump, at his suggestion, and he will give the statue to Willow Creek when it is finished. There is no special purpose to the statue — I think it has something to do with delight, and the celebration of more than the Bigfoot, but that's me talking. It just seemed like a good idea to Jim.

He plans to go on with his work, "for the rest of my life, if I have to. I'm not interested so much in proving that the *yeti* exists — I'm sure that'll happen in my time — as I am in what happens afterward, when the lawyers and the anthropologists get going. If the *yetis* aren't human, they can be hunted and killed like any animal, and if they are — well, either way they'll need to be protected. That's what concerns me."

Later this month, he and a few friends will be going on a two-week expedition in search of the Bigfoot. There will be others next year; hopefully, several simultaneous expeditions in different parts of the country. He asks us to keep this first one secret, though he has no great hopes for its success. "If we don't find anything, you'll probably hear a lot about it — but if we should, just by luck, we'll try to keep it as quiet as possible. The real work will begin then."

The range of the coast redwood begins at the Oregon border and runs down into Mendocino County before the trees begin to thin out. They grow inland as far as 50 miles, depending on the extent of the fog belt. Coast redwoods are taller than the Sierra sequoias, but not as massive, and they don't live as long. Along the Redwood Highway, people have groves and individual trees named for them. Traveling down 101, you come to believe that everybody along here lives off the big trees, in one way and another. The people who don't fell them corral a couple of acres fronting the Redwood Highway and build motels, resorts, restaurants, gift shops that sell redwood ashtrays and little redwood bears. The best thing is to find a couple of oddities— tree-houses, drive-thrus, whatever—and set up your pitch around them. Redwoods, perhaps because of their greedy hold on life, on any terms, have a tendency to curious deformities and grotesque survivals. The "Trees of Mystery" place is the most famous example: it features some fifteen exhibits in the old Robert Ripley manner, and with the same evasive veracity.

Comparisons between Ferndale and the coast town of Mendocino, 100 miles south, are easy and inevitable. Both towns were founded in the middle of the nineteenth century by Yankees and Portuguese (and Danish dairy farmers, in Ferndale's case). The architecture is a similar blend of lacy, fanciful softness and sudden uncompromising lines and angles—though Mendocino's New England foundation is even more obvious than Ferndale's. Mendocino has been known as an art center for the last twenty years, and Ferndale is beginning to attract its own colony of artists and writers. No one has yet shot a movie in Ferndale (Johnny Belinda, Frenchman's Creek, East of Eden, and The Russians Are Coming all made varying use of Mendocino scenery), but someone will. Both places look immediately like what they are, which is important in movies.

But Ferndale is prosperous; neat and calm with its dairy money; and Mendocino's lumber mill closed in 1938. Until the artists and the summer people began to discover it after World War II, Mendocino barely breathed in its sleep; and even now, for all the bunny-abundance of art galleries and antique shoppes, the town is officially classed as a Depressed Area. (Real-estate dealers are multiplying too—perhaps because of the new nearness of the Bay Area, and the low tax rate.) Mendocino is darker than Ferndale, and sadder to be in, and more interesting. I don't know which is the more handsome town.

Mendocino church

143

Early morning on the Ferndale–Petrolia road. If you leave Ferndale by the narrow, bad road that struggles toward Cape Mendocino, you'll pass through a quietly wonderful part of California. The towns are called Petrolia, Honeydew, Upper Mattole, Ettersburg, and they are on the Mattole River. I don't think you can always find them.

9. Something Between
a Sigh and a Snarl

(SONOMA AND NORTH COAST)

I like Sonoma County. I think I'd like to live here sometime, and I know a lot of people who have the same ambition. Most of us seem to be the sort of eternally dissatisfied people who love Marin County both for its startling beauty and its comfortable nearness to San Francisco, and who *feel* it becoming overcrowded; as though there were some kind of population clock in our stomachs. Three hundred and fifty people per square mile — and that was in the good old days this morning. It's gone up since lunchtime.

Sonoma is next north, still within easy — perhaps too easy — reach of the Bay Area, but three times as large as Marin, and with substantially less people. The country is a good deal like Marin: rolling and easy, with bright, lopsided hills. (Geographically, Sonoma County is part of the Northwest, but it has much more in common with the soft Central Coast area.) The main difference, to my mind, is that in Marin County you're always aware of the ocean, wherever you are; not only because of the weather and the wind's taste, but because the water is simply present even when you're waiting for a light to change in Fairfax. Sonoma has a coastline — a proper northwestern one, foggy and tattered — but the southern valleys have no more sense of that gray weight than an equally pastoral region of Pennsylvania would have. The climate's more like Santa Cruz, with the same cool, slow-ripening summers that suddenly flare into rich Octobers and Novembers. It's good wine weather.

Historically, Sonoma is as far north as the Spanish ever cared to go. Neither they nor the English in Canada were much interested in the California Northeast — not until the Russians established themselves on the Sonoma coast in 1812, at Fort Ross. That eventually brought the Spanish north, and then the Mexicans, after independence. By then, the Russian outpost — whose original purpose had been to raise food for the fur-traders in Alaska — was doing well enough that the Czar was encouraged to claim the northern Pacific Coast as a private preserve for Russian shipping. For twenty years, until the Russians gave up on Fort Ross, sold it to John Sutter, and went back to Alaska, the Mexicans guarded and fortified the Line of the North against invasion. The Mission San Francisco Solano and the Pueblo de Sonoma were founded during that time, and for no other reason.

Grape harvesting in the Napa Valley. California supplies 80 per cent of the wine consumed in America; and of the state's 250-odd wineries, a third are located in the relatively small region of the Napa and Sonoma valleys. Some are highly automated, with no limestone caverns and no great carved oaken doors, but the antiseptic glass-and-steel-tubing decor of any modern professional's office. Fred and Eleanor McCrea's small Stony Hill Vineyard, however, maintains the stone and the oak and the faint, dusty chill. Like all wineries today, Stony Hill employs sophisticated analytical techniques to determine the sugar, acid, alcohol, and extract content of the wines and musts; but the grapes are still crushed in a hand-operated basket press, a procedure long since outmoded in most commercial wineries. The McCreas produce only a limited amount of wine, using less than half of their grapes, and selling the rest to neighboring wineries. They sell their own Pinot Chardonnay and Gewurz Traminer entirely by mail, to a list of some 500 customers.

"It's a dangerous business," Fred McCrea says. He is a retired San Francisco advertising man: tall, gentle, and quietly, implicitly glad to have gotten here, to be living with his hills and his sea-blue grapes. "I don't mean just as a business, though it is that, of course. The kind of nice, romantic people who are attracted to winemaking are the kind who usually go broke terribly fast. But winemaking is dangerous even if you just get into it as a hobby. It's so much fun, and so complex, and such a challenge that it's easy to get pulled into this world full-time, unless your real job is comparably interesting. Most jobs aren't."

It's funny to think about Fort Ross, about the Russians being in California: trying to hear the sound of a Greek Orthodox mass in the chapel; to see the low, small, creaking room jammed with kneeling sailors — the officers probably had a separate mass — who had walked halfway across Russia and Alaska to be here, now. Imagine the miasma of steaming, stinking fur that must have clouded the room. Did the Aleuts come to mass too — the Arctic Indians who hunted sea otters for the Russians, in the California tradition of non-union labor? What did the Aleuts think, listening in the doorway?

The sailors weren't farmers; and once the sea otters and the fur seals had been killed off, everything went to hell. The colonists tried shipbuilding for a little while, but they used green timber and the ships rotted in the water. It's hard to imagine the Spanish and Mexicans — and the Americans — taking them seriously as the arrowhead of a Russian invasion, but the important point is that they did. The Mexicans invited Yankee settlers into Sonoma — the same gringos who eventually led the Bear Flag Revolt there, and who took over after California was ceded to the United States in 1848. And it was the Czar's coastal adventure, as much as anything, that elicited the Monroe Doctrine, with its warning that the hemisphere was now closed to European expansion. A lot of historical currents converged around Sonoma in the early nineteenth century, and some of them are still flowing along under our time.

But all I really know about Sonoma County these days is that there's cockfighting going on all over the place. It isn't unique to Sonoma — I'm sure I could find a pit around Santa Cruz without much trouble — but the enforcement of the law against cockfighting seems to become more stringent as you travel farther south. In one northern county, a few years back, the police raided a cockfight and confiscated all the birds — about two hundred of them. (Owning a gamecock isn't illegal, by the way; but trimming of the comb and plumage is considered evidence that the bird is going to be fought.) The cocks were tossed together into a big pen, and in the morning every one of them was dead. Their owners sued the city, charging destruction of property, and they won. That particular county has been more than usually lenient with cockfighters ever since.

Cockfighting is very old, perhaps five thousand years old as a recognized sport. It probably evolved in Asia and entered western Europe by way of Greece. The Romans knew it, and the Egyptians. There can hardly be a nation on earth where cockfghting hasn't flourished at one time or another (there is a legend that the gamecock missed becoming the American bird by one vote), and very few where it has ever been successfully suppressed. It is still the national sport of the Philippine Islands; and on the West Coast, cockfighting is almost entirely a Filipino concern. The Anglos here generally pick it up from Filipinos who work for them or with them. Oddly, there don't seem to be many Mexicans involved in cockfighting.

Most of the people who raise gamecock and fight them are farmers or field workers; though I'm sure that there are streets deep in San Francisco, Los Angeles, Stockton, Sacramento, where — if the traffic would only be still for a moment — you could catch the

Fort Ross

clattering four-note challenges, *cock-a-DOO-doo*, unmistakable, soaring from a cellar or a rooftop. They are always men, usually middle-aged, and sometimes very old. Young people come to the fights and bet on the birds, but it's not the same thing for them. They are growing up with movies and TV and radios, with freeways, as the old men grew up with the birds. Still, I know an eleven-year-old Mexican boy named Jaime who travels up and down the coast with his father on weekends, fighting their birds. They live in King City, where Jaime's father works as a crop-sprayer. Jaime has been traveling with the cocks since he was eight.

The birds themselves are beautiful with purpose, in the way of a wild thing, not a barn-yard animal. When you hold them, they feel hard and heavy as hand grenades; and yet it is also like holding a delicate kite that lifts in your hands when the smallest wind blows. A gamecock may be any color, from a deep black with purple highlights to the speckly

Weigh-in for a cockfight

gray or yellowish-white of stale snow. The most beautiful one I ever saw was a White-hackle, the kind they call red. He was actually a bursting, buttery orange, except for his underbody near the legs, which was blue and green-black. His neck feathers were brighter than the rest of his body — molten gold in the sunlight — and they lay down along his shoulders like a mane, distinct from the feathers beneath. But he wasn't nearly the fighter that he looked and felt, and he was dead within thirty seconds of the time that he was set down in the pit.

Slasher fights, such as this one was, usually last anywhere from five seconds to a minute. In slasher fighting, each bird is armed with a knife like a miniature Spanish sword, two to four inches in length, as a rule, though there is no limit. The knife is tied to the sawed-off stump of the cock's natural spur — an art in itself, that may take fifteen minutes to complete, between the padding and fitting of the knife, and the separate bindings of thread and tape and thread again. It's said that only one man out of three or four hundred knows how to tie properly; and even master cockfighters, totally knowledgeable about every other aspect of the game, will often take their own birds to such a specialist. If the cock wins, the tier is entitled to a piece of the purse.

There is another style of fighting, with long, curved tines called gaffs. These matches can go on for an hour, even two two hours. Anglos favor the gaffs, while the Filipinos, by and large, won't have anything to do with them. The difference is not between two weapons, but two worlds.

Because of the length of gaff fights, the winner is almost always the better bred and conditioned bird. Therefore, the kings among the Anglo cockfighters are the men who plan their birds generations at a time, paying infinite attention to such details as the mineral and animal content of the soil on which a particular cock is to be raised (like the old Nantucket captains who were supposed to be able to pinpoint their ships' locations by tasting the sea). They blend different types of birds as winemakers cross and graft grapes. Whitehackles, Kelsos, Wisconsin Red Shufflers, Madigan Grays, Minor Blues, Clarets, Mugs — this for speed, that for power, this much for a high-flying attack, that for cutting ability. Each man has his own secret conditioning methods: certain special exercises, certain diets at four weeks and two weeks before a fight. The pages of the cockfighting magazines (*Feathered Warrior, The Gamelock, Grit and Steel*) are filled with ads for infallible conditioners and homemade vitamin supplements. Nothing is left to luck.

The Filipinos, on the other hand, court luck, and are utterly casual about the rest of it. They know good birds, and often buy shrewdly from skilled breeders, but they are much more likely to be influenced by a portentous pattern of scales on the cock's legs than by his ancestry. Dreams matter, and so do numbers and colors; what happens to be lucky today may be impotent next Sunday. Gaff fighting, with its written rules and its point system, holds no interest for most Filipinos. Slasher matches, if you watch long enough, become a ballet of community standing and relationships. This man's word is accepted absolutely in any dispute, while another can't make himself heard. This one can get away with declaring his opponent's bird dead and walking off with his own dead bird dangling; another man wouldn't dare. It looks friendly and informal, but it's actually surprisingly subtle, and it's not all that friendly.

I've never been to a gaff pit, but I've seen a number of slasher fights. They were all held on large ranches belonging to Anglos — another reason for the relative toleration of cock-fighting in the northern counties is that a good many wealthy ranchers are involved. Some of the pits have been in operation for thirty years or more.

In the south, I've heard, the fights have to be held at night, and there is a system of pass-words, and sentinels with walkie-talkies checking out darkened cars. Here, it's about as open as the neighborhood picnic it resembles, with children chasing each other and nice, motherly ladies ladling out goat stew and sweet rice in the shade. The stranger is observed closely the first few times, but people aren't obsessed with betrayal. There is a tension in the air, beneath the high spirits and the courtesy, but that's not the reason.

The matches and side bets are arranged at a weighing table. Everything else being equal — and the secret called *gameness* that keeps a cock from dying for a few seconds longer being as unfathomable and unprogramable as it has ever been — the odds favor the heavier bird. No man gives away two or three ounces casually, unless he thinks he knows some-thing. The bettors judge the cocks as they pose on the padded scales, assigning their own values to eagerness and flaring wings, to screaming and silence. It helps a lot to hold the cock for a little, but that is absolutely taboo. You never touch someone else's bird — partly because cocks sometimes get nobbled that way, but also just because it's bad luck. I've seen matches called off for that reason, without argument, even after all the bets were down.

It's hard to say how much money changes hands at a cockfight. In Florida, one of the few states where it's legal, and the big gamblers can come in openly, $750,000 has been known to cross the tables in one Orlando weekend. Here, of course, most of the purses are "small money," which is anything under a hundred dollars. But in the afternoon, when the big birds, the "shakes," start to show up, the purses may run as high as four or five hundred dollars. The book bets, taken in the pit, are always even money; and the amount wagered on both birds has to be equal before the fight can start. The bookmaker walks back and forth till then, shouting, "This side! I need forty dollars this side! Forty dollars this side!" He almost always gets it, even if the underbird really looks like an instant loser. Somebody will cover the bet, just for the hell of it.

The real money is in the side betting, because of that for-the-hell-of-it thing. As the rhythm of the day builds up, the bets get bigger and the odds get wilder: eight to five, thirty to twenty, fifty to twenty. Everybody bets, from old men with stained, apparently endless rolls in their sweater pockets, to kids with a dollar to shoot — both of them very often willing to take either side. A few are professionals, smoky-cold as dry ice in the tumult (there's one cheerful little gambler who drives a Cadillac and reputedly supports two families with his winnings); but most people just like to bet. Between matches, many

Livestock show at Marin-Sonoma Fair

will circulate around a table in the shade, where a game played with dice and huge amber dominoes will be going on all day. It adds up to a lot of money in a full day — real money, earned picking lettuce and prunes. They chance it lightly, but that's part of the fierceness all the same.

The handlers will be in the pit while the betting is going on, letting their birds see each other. They bring the cocks head to head, pull them away, shove them together again, while the birds scream in frustration and peck viciously at combs and heads. A cock that won't peck is grounds enough for canceling the match right there, but it hardly ever happens. This is what they are for. All those thousands of years of selective breeding have produced a completely separate strain of game fowl, further removed from a barnyard bird than a black Miura bull is from a polled Hereford. The handlers remove the long scabbards, tasseled and curved like jesters' shoes, from the cocks' heels. They toss the birds down.

The cocks attack in long, high hops, silent now, except for the whicking of their wings. Their neck feathers are standing straight up, making their throats look skinny and raw.

Sometimes they spring clear over one another, and sometimes their breasts meet in a soft explosion of dust, with their curled legs raking. Even when they seem to have missed each other entirely, one knife may suddenly show red to the mounting; though the wounded cock leaps as high as ever, and does not fall then. But something between a sigh and a snarl passes over the pit at the sight of the first blood, and a few men grunt as though the little knife had struck into them.

First blood is no assurance of victory; not even the dark, slow, ropy blood from the beak that always means a lung wound. Nor is the fight over when one cock is a heap of damp, dimming feathers on the ground, and the other bird is untouched and preening for the kill. The undeniable power of the cockfight is that anything can happen until death — and sometimes, seemingly, for a little while after the death. A gamecock will be stabbing out when every other reflex in him has ceased to function. This is what they are for.

The one real rule of slasher fighting has to do with this fact, that it is not easy to tell when a gamecock is dead. The handler of an obviously beaten cock may try to keep the match going while there is the smallest evidence of life left in his bird: shouting, "*Carrio!*" when a wing twitches after minutes of stillness, and putting the bird on its feet, to flurry forward (often with amazing fury) and collapse again. Generally, he isn't holding out with any hope of victory, but for a *tabla*, a draw, in which case all bets would be off. Since the odds are very good that both birds will die, the chances of a *tabla* increase with every minute. It may also happen that the winner fails to deliver the ritual peck on the loser's head, and that means a *tabla* too. Sometimes he's too exhausted to make it; but often it's because he knows the other bird is dead, if nobody else does. Cocks have absolutely no interest in dead birds.

It's very much a matter of style and standing, as I've said. There is never an official referee, as in the gaff fights; but in time you come to recognize certain old men who are always in the pit when the handlers have shooed everyone else out, and whose word represents the judgment of the community, unassailable. It works — a "kill-the-umpire" mob scene just doesn't happen, however much money may be at stake — but it is from this center that the tension soaks into the atmosphere of a cockfight. For all the politeness and laughter, the long friendships, the picnic feeling, the family feeling, something even older than the instincts and reflexes of the chickens is on trial in the pit. I only sense it occasionally, with the hairs on my arms, but it's there all the time.

Killings are very rare, but not unheard of. I know of one case, concerning a Filipino man who wandered into a gaff fight and got into an argument with a Mexican. The Filipino didn't know the rules, or the complicated point system, and he accused the other man of cheating. What he said, actually, was, "You no sport. You no play sport here." The Mexican pulled out a pistol and shot him dead.

That really is the worst thing you can say — *You no play sport here*. I've only heard it said once at a cockfight, and there was death crackling that time too, though nothing happened. A man who was at the gaff fight where the Filipino was shot explains it this way:

State Capitol, Sacramento

154

"It's challenge and answer, just like the chickens. You say this, he says that, click-click-click. Most times, somebody can stop it — break up the pattern, you know — before it gets too far. It's not hard. But this time, the pattern just went right along to the end, click-click-click. And the life didn't mean a thing. You remember that. The life didn't mean a thing."

I never paid much mind to Hemingway when he said things like, ". . . this honor thing is not some fantasy I am trying to inflict on you. I swear it is true." Hemingway and his bulls, and his murdered rhinoceroses. My man has always been Falstaff, catechizing himself on the morning of battle. "What is honor? A word. What is in that word honor? What is that honor? Air . . . . Therefore I'll none of it. Honor is a mere scutcheon." Falstaff is the modern man of the two; the only safe man for our time, while the generals are still booming and babbling about honor. *Click-click-click.*

But Hemingway did know something real, after all. I have seen a little of what he knew in the worn, worn, kind faces of the gentle old men when the cocks are whipping in the dirt; when they tumble out of the pit, bound together by one bird's knife sunk between the other's wings, and the circle of watchers makes a new pit where they fall. We recoil from knowing this, and it's probably just as well. I think there are one or two things in man that we do damn well to deny.

But our well-brought-up children — intelligent, beautiful, never hungry, never frustrated — often go wandering out at night, five or six together, and they kick people to death; they set them on fire, they beat their heads in and leave them on the beach, or lying across the streetcar tracks. And when we catch them and ask them why they did it, they always answer, "I don't know."

We have no legal blood sports in this country — except boxing, if you like, and that may very well disappear in our time. We confuse that with having no need for blood. I'd go to a dozen cockfights (or even a dogfight; they exist in most states too, though they're much harder to find) before I'd go to the average Hollywood movie these days. I still don't have much feeling for honor, but it's better than that terrible *nothing*. It's better than "I don't know."

10. Everyone Was Twenty-two

(BERKELEY)

Berkeley, Berkeley. I lived here once. It was only for a couple of months in the summer of 1961, but it seems longer now. That's probably because I made three friends that summer, which is full half the number you may dare to hope for in a lifetime, according to the Irish writer A.E. For several years afterward, most of the people in California that I cared about still lived in Berkeley, and so I knew some part of what was going on in the town, and kept a good feeling for it. I still have that feeling, though I know very few people in Berkeley now.

I would like to write something about that time, just to get it down. Does anybody remember 1961? That was a good summer. Kennedy had only been in office for a few months, and Mort Sahl was already somewhat *passé*. Sahl was a Berkeley boy, with a wit, developed over the tables at Robbie's on Telegraph Avenue, that cut like a black fin through the stagnant fifties. But in 1961, for a little while, humor growing out of the fact that nothing changes and that hope is hypocrisy really seemed irrelevant. For a little while. The Freedom Riders went South that summer — who remembers the Freedom Riders? My brother was eighteen, and he wanted to go with them. The Peace Corps meant something; and so did America's admission that Americans, black and white, were starving in 1961. Nobody had ever heard of Vietnam, and there weren't many who understood the message of the Bay of Pigs. That happened so fast, anyway, and it just didn't go with that brief, expectant time, that sense of having broken the old cycles. Who remembers? I swear I'm not making it up. I was twenty-two then — everyone was twenty-two.

Hemingway killed himself that summer. I saw the headline as I was walking down Telegraph. "Striding," we called it — just striding the Avenue, strolling in and out of all the bookstores, Moe's and U.C. Corner, and Cody's (farther down the block then, and a much smaller place); reading the posters at the double-barreled movie house that Pauline Kael used to run; checking in at the Piccolo (officially the Mediterraneum, but I only hear it called that these days), which had taken over from Robbie's around the beginning of the sixties, as the place to sit around and wait for everybody to come by. Watching the girls, watching the Berkeley girls, the ones who seemed to be spending the summer luxuriating in their own potential before they chose anything. A real stride, a dedicated professional, could spend all day every day within four blocks on Telegraph, weighing the heavy decision of what party to make that night. There was always a party somewhere.

Red wine and Ray Charles, and me trapped on a mattress with my back to the wall and my legs sticking straight out. People still played the bongos at parties. Lots of smoke, and some of it the sweet, lazy smell of marijuana. Pot was so available that it was easy to forget that it wasn't legal. Yet there wasn't a heavy drug scene in Berkeley, as there is now. Granted, LSD hadn't yet fallen from heaven, but the hallucinogens like *yage* and psilocybin were already familiar, and some of the pillheads were beginning on methedrine. But I don't think many people were shooting up, getting hooked — it was considered pointless and square. That's changed.

Fantastic clothing simply didn't exist then. Today, of course, you can sit in front of the Forum, which was a supermarket in 1961, and study a dizzyingly pied and scrambled spectrum of disguises, ranging from Buffalo Bill to Count Dracula, and sometimes combining the best elements of both. But in those days, Az pretty much had the fancy dress market cornered, with his shoulder-length yellow hair, his monk's habit, rope belt, and pilgrim's staff. He said that his name was short for Azazel, and that he was about two thousand years old. A pleasant cat, on the whole. He vanished forever one day, and the word went around that he was really the son of an Oakland industrialist, who had been paying him a sizable allowance to stay away from home Until; and that Until had finally arrived. Azazel. He wouldn't be noticed on Telegraph today, if he returned from Oakland.

I don't mean that there weren't any costumes at all. There always are, but the strangely innocent styles of the time laid great emphasis on not looking like costumes. It was the last round for proletarian dress; seasoned somewhat with the *On the Road* look. Checked flannel shirts, neckerchiefs, sheepskin jackets. Wandering was in, but so was working on the railroad and following the crops. Woody Guthrie and Kerouac. All that seems to be left of that ensemble is the brakeman's hat (because of Dylan) and the wire-rimmed spectacles, and some of the buckskin fringe. The clothes may come back, but I don't think the attitude will.

It all tied in with the folk music, of course — the big wave really came in that year. There had been a surge of interest in folk singing in the late 1930s, and then there was the Burl Ives-Josh White-Woody Guthrie-Leadbelly-Weavers revival that came after the war. I grew up with that one, and I was always involved with folk music in a casual kind of way. It never died out, but it was something you had to look for, and it was a very small world. There were little folk groups at most colleges, and that was it.

But that third wave! This time, it was more than a revival — for a while, it was a way of life. That's important to remember. Think of it: thousands and thousands of kids singing seriously about Geordie, and the Twa Corbies, and Fair Ellender; about mean ol' cap'ns, mojo teeth and seventh sons, and falling in wi' a fairmer sheel by the barnyards o' Delgaty. College students of impeccable liberal persuasion were making thousand-mile treks into the Cumberland and Smoky backwoods to learn variant versions of sixteenth-century murder ballads from creepy, bigoted, old white Southerners. They tracked the vanished bluesmen of twenty, thirty, forty years gone — Bukka White, Son House, Skip James —

Steps of Sproul Hall, U. C. Berkeley

from the Mississippi delta to the soft, dank apartments on Chicago's South Side, and back down again to the shacks built on four piles of stones in Memphis, Nashville — all to tape-record them and bring them out to California, to the folk festivals and the folk coffee-houses. Everybody was coming to Berkeley.

How can I explain what I mean by a way of life? I used to know people who did nothing else but travel the folk circuit, which had its main treminals in Berkeley, Chicago — maybe Denver — Ann Arbor, Boston, and New York. Some were legends, coming and going: king folkies like Perry Lederman, Billy "Twelvestring" Roberts, Spider John Koerner,

Marc Silber, Steve Talbot; some were journeymen and less, amateurs who filled in on the programs, got to do one or two numbers at parties, and occasionally begged into guest sets at the Blind Lemon or the Cabale. To these you have to add the collectors, who'd sit around all night playing their tapes at each other and arguing about field hollers and Child ballads; and the lovely, dangerous little folk chicks, who played some themselves, if they looked good that way, but mostly just went with folk singers, and only folk singers; and all those pale teen-agers with no apparent homes or families, expressionlessly picking their New York Martins with unbelievable skill and sureness, the bass driving, the treble strings singing and stinging. Most of that was nothing but motor reflexes, but it sure floored me. I never did learn to play *Freight Train*.

The girls were just coming off Odetta's repertoire and starting to sing Joan Baez. The boys did a lot of Guthrie, Leadbelly, Ewan MacColl, all-purpose Theodore Bikel European, and the New Lost City Ramblers' Depression stuff. The bluegrass bag was fine for the banjo players, but it doomed a lot of good guitarists to three-chord backups and occasional Lester Flatt runs in G. Kids who wanted to play the blues used to hang out with mentors, in a sort of monk-*chela* relationship, trying to get at the secret, the life under the music, as well as what Brownie McGhee, Jesse Fuller, or Blind Gary Davis did with it. That's gone now, that time of white apprentices running errands for old Negro musicians. That's just gone.

Everybody was making records, even if they had to start up their own record companies to do it. The big companies were actively in the market, and it really seemed awfully easy to land a contract at one point. But only one guy out of that scene ever truly made it: Jim Kweskin, who's still doing very well with his jug band. There were a dozen guitarists as good or better around Berkeley then, but Kweskin was the one who stuck with folk when the others got out of it. Malvina Reynolds, who's been writing songs for twenty years, hit with "Little Boxes" and "What Have They Done to the Rain?"; and Jeannie Redpath, who was in Berkeley that summer, went on to make a couple of beautiful albums in New York. But there never was that much money in folk music, except for the promoters and the midwives. The real attraction was the folk life.

You could be somebody else. Each kind of music implied the kind of person who would sing it, and you could pick the music you felt best being. My own bag was French *chansonnier* stuff, and I know I still become different when I sing Brassens or Ferré. It was the same for other people, I think. Some were self-made Okies, like Ramblin' Jack Elliot; others became wild Celts, hobos, Spanish gypsies, Negroes of all colors. There were some poor souls who floundered sadly between ill-fitting images, trying on a different one at each party; but in time you could usually find your music, your secret name. Shel Silverstein wrote a good song about all that. "But what do you do if you're young and white and Jewish?"

It's about vanished, as a life. It was fading well before Bob Dylan (who turned up scuffling in the Village that same winter — they used to call him "Lockjaw Dylan" at

This isn't the evangelist who usually patrols Sather Gate at U.C. Berkeley. The regular preacher is named Hubert. I've seen him there for several years, any chance noon that I'm there: late thirties, red hair, shiny freckled face, long flat fingers, tireless voice, and eyes that always look between the eyes or over the shoulder of the person with whom he's arguing. The students are generally very courteous to Hubert. They don't like anything he stands for, doubtless, but they can comprehend him as a single man.

Gerde's Folk City) came on with his electric guitar at the Newport Festival in 1965. Everybody knew all the songs. All the old guitars and banjos had been scoured out of every attic in the country. Inevitably, people got tried of worrying about whether they sounded "ethnic" and "authentic" enough. It wasn't just the acoustic Martin and Gibson guitars that gave way to the Fenders and Rickenbackers, to all that electronic equipment that looks like the bomber cockpit in *Dr. Strangelove*. What really went out was the old romantic image of the wandering ballad singer, and what replaced it was the concept of the rock band: city boys, superhip, yet vulnerable; living and working together, creating the folk songs and *lieder* of this time, this moment — there aren't any generations anymore. I like the music, but I'm too old to change of my fantasies. That's the real dividing line between one time and another — the out-of-date daydream.

The music left its logical mark, though. A lot of the young rock musicians playing now came out of the folk scene, and sometimes I catch echoes of the runs and chord changes and three-finger riffs that were standards in 1961. I get very excited then, and start explaining the music to my wife and fifteen-year-old daughter. James Dickey titles a book of poems *Buckdancer's Choice*, and I grin knowingly. You had to be good to play that tune. See, I do like rock, but I don't really care.

That was a good summer, anyway, listening to the music. It ended with the Berlin crisis in August. The draft boards stepped up their calls, the reservists were called back in, the ones who could duck back into school did; and within a couple of weeks Telegraph seemed suddenly shorn of all the young men, all the strides. Things never truly eased off again — the way the price of orange juice has never come back down since the cold winter five years ago. I sometimes find myself looking back on that tiny era the way people are forever writing about the good years from 1900 to 1914. They thought it was a beginning, but it was an end.

Delta Country

11. There Is a Loneliness

(DELTA COUNTRY)

Northeast of San Francisco Bay is the delta country, where the Sacramento and San Joaquin rivers join. If you drew a triangle whose apices were at Sacramento, Stockton, and Vallejo, you'd contain most of the delta within it. Mike and I went up there in a 36-foot sloop, the *Alanya*, captained by Larry Jay, a friend of Mike's from Sausalito. We sailed her across San Pablo Bay, past Pittsburg and Port Chicago, the Navy explosives town; past the bellowing mills of Antioch, and the endless ghostly line of World War II carriers being reconditioned for Vietnam, and so up the San Joaquin.

The delta is a strange place, attractive and dull at the same time. It is unrelievedly flat, like Belgium or the Netherlands, and like the Netherlands it is reclaimed land. The Chinese raised it out of the river in the 1870's, after they built the railroads, and for about the same wages. They used wheelbarrows and shovels, and they built up a system of dikes and levees that made it possible to farm land lying well below water level. The soil is peat, black and deeply fertile, and the delta produces million-dollar crops of sugar beets, tomatoes, asparagus, almonds, walnuts, apricots, pears, peaches, and prunes. There are natural gas fields here too, around Rio Vista, and many farmers in the area now live entirely off their mineral royalties.

The sloughs are inevitably compared to the Everglades, which really isn't fair. There is nothing in the least untamed or dramatic about the thousand miles of waterways that meander through the delta, lined by willows and cottonwoods and the ubiquitous tule grass with the little tassels on top. It's not a good place to do nothing: you have to fish, or water-ski, or blast around in a powerboat, for the region itself won't nourish you for long. All the same, the slough country has a curious, rather fragile charm, like its pale, finespun sunsets.

The towns along the sloughs are unexciting, and yet — like the land — a little haunting. Rio Vista is the biggest town, and the wealthiest, and the least interesting; but dry, shallow places like Walnut Grove, and Locke, and Isleton are good for walking around. In Walnut Grove, the markets and cafes, garages and marine supply stores, and the inevitable art gallery are all lined out on the high street along the levee; but once you slope down into the town, it's all narrow streets and gray, exhausted frame houses, and people popping in and out of boarded-up storefronts. Old Chinese and Filipino men sit on boxes and benches on a corner, letting everything go by, but looking at it. A large

165

young white man in a sweaty white shirt is going slowly from one door of a barrackslike building to the next, collecting money from Mexicans.

Mr. Singh lives down in the scoop of the town, in his package store, with his bed and a little stove. Mike and I went in there, because Singh is the name that Sikhs take — it means "Lion" — and I wanted to see what one of those fierce, handsome, bearded people was doing running a liquor store in Walnut Grove. But he was small and bent, with a terribly naked face, splotched with blue, flesh pulling away from the eyes and mouth. Mr. Singh is dying in Walnut Grove, and he wanted us to go away and leave him alone, so we went away.

Walnut Grove is sad after a while; but Locke, which is even smaller and more silent, and where even less is going on, wears much better. The difference may lie in the fact that Locke is more truly out of time than Walnut Grove is. The only tourist attraction in town is a bumptious Irish bar called "Al the Wop's." Outside of that, the town belongs to the old men, to the cats, and to the old, old houses; so old that they cannot be said to be crumbling or decaying any more. They are past ruin: they have melted together into a special gracefulness and dignity, with their swooping roofs, their buckled balconies, their false fronts like tombstones. The sidewalks are wooden, as gray and soft as the houses.

On an archway between two of the houses, the pale block letters say STAR THEATRE. But there is no building under the arch — there is nothing but the sea-dim alley, the broken stairways, the water pipes, the houses' sides bulging like cows' sides. What did they show in the Star Theatre? And who came to see it? And why is it not just closed but gone? What shows did they give in the Star Theatre, how long ago?

"I wonder what it's like to live here." Larry and Mike and I are sitting on a porch in company with two comfortably silent Chinese men. It is very hot, ninety in the shade. There is a smell of incense coiling out of the shuttered house at our backs. "What's it like to grow up here?" It is my eternal question about any strange town, though I didn't realize it until Mike called me on it the other day, in some other town.

"It's not a bad place to be old in," Larry says, "or very young. Little kids have a great time running around in places like this, or Walnut Grove. It's not even so bad to be fourteen, fifteen, and wanting to get out. But it's hell on the women. It's an awful place to be a woman."

I'd never done any real sailing before this trip. It's a maddeningly slow way to get anywhere. Two or three miles in an hour sometimes, and less than that if the wind fails; nothing to do but feel yourself frying, tug on the halyards till you can't close your hands, keep a wary eye on the depth sounder that's showing nine feet of water when the chart says a clear sixteen; duck the boom when it comes swinging over as you tack and wallow to find the wind, and brace yourself when one of those damn monstrous powerboats goes by. Don't get your face fixed for electricity at the marina, or showers either.

But the thing about sailing is that getting there isn't nearly as important as getting there without using the motor. The real joy is in the navigating, in plotting your course

Fishing for catfish in Delta

and playing the wind, the tide, and the current to make them take you where you want to go. The delight is in being small and utterly powerless, and still using them. As for the slowness of it: after a little time, it is the insanity of going seventy, fifty, or even thirty miles an hour that amazes you. Distance begins to have meaning again, which is odd in California.

Everything that floats can be met on the sloughs: ocean-going ships bound up the deep-water channel for Sacramento; homemade boats without bottoms, steered with a piece of wood, rigged with rags, proudly recapitulating the earliest beginnings of sailing ships; rowboats with outboard motors clipped on behind, and strange, lean, frail craft powered by vast automobile engines. Rented houseboats come chugging along, looking like the embodiment of a lazy Sunday morning. There's a powerboat berthed in Rio Vista that cost around $300,000 to fit out. It looks as big as a duplex, and it's equipped with everything from a 5000-gallon fuel tank to its own desalinating system. We passed three boys floating down Steamboat Slough on a door.

Several yacht clubs have bought islands in the sloughs and keep them up all year round as private resorts. We stayed at one for a couple of days. It was beautiful and well-kept, and the people were friendly, and their children were handsome and charming, and they had some great old boats, and after two days I was counting my toes and picking uncontrollably at the anchor cable. The place felt like Sartre's *No Exit*.

Larry said, "You have to take it for what it is." Larry works as a bookkeeper for Crown Zellerbach, and reads Cervantes and Unamuno in the original, and knows a lot of things in between. "These guys aren't old, big rich; they work for their money, and they work at the kind of job that wears you out from the inside, while you sit there. They come up here to do just what they do — sleep, fish, drink, sail, and mainly not answer the telephone. There isn't a telephone on this island. It's that kind of place."

He's right; but there's something lonely and dull and distant about the island. The houseboats that are kept here all year round look exactly like tract homes in Pacifica. I think of the bright, crazy-quilt houseboats rotting happily in Sausalito. Grown men talk with hushed seriousness of a friend who waited thirty-four years to get into Bohemian Grove; and a sad man, soft with Jack Daniels at eleven in the morning, says querulously, "Well, I don't mind — I'd *like* the Negroes to have things . . ."

The boats were beautiful, though. There was a big schooner, sixty years old; broad-beamed as Queen Victoria, but golden and stately as any lioness, and with an animal's quality of being all one thing, crouching there under the fractions and fragments who drank cocktails on the deck. There was one young girl — seventeen or so — sailing on that boat who had that same air. Her name was Hoppy.

The best time was an evening when we arrived twenty minutes too late for a bridge that closed at five o'clock. There wasn't a thing to do but anchor in the river for the night. Mike and I rowed ashore in the life raft and bought steak and wine for dinner in a town called Terminous. After dinner, the three of us sat out on deck and watched the evening.

Up and down the slough it was all tule and willows, and a few houses backed into the tasseled grass, the way the little boats tie up to fish. The sunset was subtle and restrained, as always on the sloughs — light pink, pale green. Three or four young boys came down to swim near the bridge. Their voices sounded like light rain on the water.

It was the water tower that made the evening, I think. It stood up on the Terminous shore near a long, dark building on pilings that might have been a cannery. The tower was roan-colored in the darkening air, dimpled and dented, shaped like a huge steam whistle. And yet it had a gracefulness, rising there on the shadowy Z's of its girders; and there was something about it that didn't have to be there to make it work better. This may only be liberal sentimentality about rust, but that evening it was easy to imagine someone having taken pride in that tower thirty years ago; some engineer backing off and saying, "By God, that's a good-looking tower. That really is a good-looking tower."

You see, it was so quiet. There were insect sounds, and the water under the bows, and the sound of the anchor cables as the boat swung between them. Trucks went by on both shores, and once a jet formation flew over, blinking and glowing like deep-sea things; but the noises seemed no louder than the voices of the swimming boys. The moon came up over the tower, and it was almost the same color.

There is a loneliness in the look of America that will never go away, no matter what we do to the land. I think sometimes that the frenzy with which we gouge and fill, level and pave, build and build and build, grows out of our need to tear down the places where the loneliness lives, to destroy the natural habitat of the creature. But it adapts itself to the things we make, and flourishes in them in direct proportion to our efforts to abolish it. It can live in a water tower as easily as in a mountain; cut down a thousand-year-old grove of redwoods, and it springs up in Daly City. It is our daemon and our muse. That's why we have the great photographers, and a lot of poets.

Coming down through Willow Creek another time, we stop to check on Jim McClarin. The statue is there, almost completed, but still rough and blocky down one side. It still looks like a gorilla. Jim isn't there; we didn't really expect him to be. The fall term must have begun at Humboldt State. It might be fun to stop off in Arcata and find out what happened on the Bigfoot hunt.

But by chance — mainly because I'm trying to find a toy stuffed elephant, which is impossible between San Francisco and Portland — we go into a little department store right across the highway. No elephant, but the manager turns out to be an old friend of Jim McClarin's — indeed, the one who first gave him Ivan Sanderson's snowman book. I should have known it by the plaster casts of huge tracks hanging on the wall. Come to think of it, the nice lady who is the tourist information service in Weaverville had a few of those hanging up too, and she really believed in the Bigfoot. That's a real underground, not like the newspapers.

"No, Jim's still up in Vancouver, looking at the film. He called up last night. Oh. Well, you fellows don't know about the Bigfoot film, do you?"

It happened a week ago, quite near Willow Creek, while Jim was still out in the back country. The man who stumbled on the *yeti* certainly wasn't looking for it, but by chance he had a movie camera in his saddlebag when his horse ran right up on the Bigfoot. The horse promptly spooked and fell, and the Bigfoot fled, but the man followed as far as he could, and the camera hadn't been damaged. The film was shipped to Vancouver to be developed, primarily because the university there has been interested in Bigfoot research for some time. When Jim returned from his own unrewarding search, he went immediately to Vancouver himself.

"Jim said when he called that the film's pretty bouncy and blurry, because the fellow was running and just shooting blind, but he says it's a real picture. The clearest one anybody's ever gotten of a Bigfoot. Apparently the people up there are real excited about it."

He's calm himself, but obviously as proud of Jim as though it were he who had sighted the Bigfoot and shot the film. Jim had never seen a *yeti* until then; did it look anything like his statue, or his sheaf of drawings?

"Well, it's funny. He said it didn't look very much the way he thought it would, but he wasn't too specific. It's a female, and it ran on its hind legs all the time, and he didn't say a lot more than that. One thing — he's changed his mind about it being some kind of human being. He's pretty sure it's an ape, one of the great apes. I always thought it must be."

San Diego Zoo

People at Play

Hell's Angel

California Palace of the Legion of Honor

Hippie in tree, Golden Gate Park

Opening night of the San Francisco opera season. This was the best part of it, the scene from a Depression comedy: the long black cars pulling up one by one, and real chauffeurs hopping out and hustling around back to open the door, and maybe tuck a stole around Madame's gleaming shoulders and glittering throat. The women were distant enough to look misty and beautiful; and we were the murmuring crowd, drawn together by our wonder and our cloth caps; hungry and shivering, but not malicious, knowing that one of us was Gary Cooper or William Powell.

Inside, it was pretty awful. Men can get away with looking like hell—especially in tailcoats—but women haven't a chance. Terrible casting obvious, heavy-handed. I don't know what Sturges can have been thinking of. Where's Rosalind Russell?

Marineland

Golden Gate Park Hippie

Governor Reagan

Boardwalk, Santa Cruz

Dune Buggy

This is a dune buggy doing a "wheely." If you do this coming over the round of a hill, the buggy may bounce clean off the ground with all four wheels. It may also go over backwards, for the frames are as light and hollow as lawn chairs, and almost all of the engines are rear-mounted. The buggies rarely get going faster than twenty-five miles an hour in the sand; but from inside, naked as a hermit crab, it feels like seventy on the wrong side of the road. Many are powered by huge eight-cylinder Ford and Buick motors, though VWs are popular because they don't overheat. You can build a buggy for fifty dollars, or a couple of thousand.

Dune-buggying has been going on in Southern California for about ten years. The Imperial Vally Dune Buggy Association, founded in 1961, estimates that 15,000 people are involved in the sport. The people that Mike and I met at Osborne Park (which is a strip of asphalt and a toilet in the desert, twenty miles east of Brawley) were mainly from the San Diego area: young carpenters, plumbers, and electricians who had driven out to the dunes on Friday night, towing the buggies on home-made trailers. Most had brought their wives and children with them. It's a uniquely American thing in several ways. The buggies are mostly home-made (though there's at least one man building frames to order now), and, like the custom cars, they express the radical personal tastes in balance and design of people for whom Art is something museums have. In the second place, there's always something that has to be fixed, tightened up, replaced, retuned. This is very important, apart from the fact that it allows room for sociability and helpfulness between strangers. Cars that run perfectly all the time really don't interest Americans. They like those pit stops. In the third place, you don't actually go anywhere. Some dune buggy people do go camping with their machines, exploring the desert or volunteering for rescue work; but the majority just run up and down the sand hills all weekend, and then drive the two or three hundred miles home. All the new American pastimes are like that, from motorboating to skydiving.

Squaw Valley above Lake Tahoe

Bird Watching

Bull Boat Race

Fort Cronkite Light

12. A Kind of Beauty
That Comforts

(MARIN AND SYNANON)

I might never have gotten to know Sausalito, if it hadn't been for this book. Mike has lived in Sausalito for ten years, in an old house under the boardwalk, on the water. Before I had ever been there, he told me, "Around your house, the dominant sound is of birds carrying on, and children. At our place, it's the bay, slooshing around under the pilings, and sort of pacing back and forth all the time." Every time I go down to Sausalito, the sound and the knowledge of the bay fill me for the first couple of days; and even when I'm not thinking about it, I'm ready, and I often wake in the night and lie listening to the water, though it's always quiet then. It's like that when you live with children.

Unless you live there, Sausalito is Bridge Way, the waterfront street that stoops from 101 just after you cross the Golden Gate Bridge. It isn't the only street in town, but because of Sausalito's peculiar topography it might as well be. Above Bridge Way, the land goes straight up, sometimes folding on itself to form natural terraces and tiny, flowered valleys; fine for houses, but impossible as a business district. So everything has to be on Bridge Way, until it trails off beyond the yacht harbor and vanishes into U.S. 101 again. The effect is quite a lot like living in a classic feudal town, looking up from the blacksmith cobblestones to the homes on the hillside and the baron's castle.

Squeezing between the bay and the hill, Bridge Way is one of the very few streets I know that can be said to have character. From the boardwalk to Ondine's is a quarter-mile walk along open water, past the skinny, silly beach, and the sillier seal statue — just plopped down there in the stony shallows, looking absurdly pleased with itself — watching sails and seagulls, and sometimes the fog, which doesn't come on little cat feet at all, but rumbles in under the Bridge with a sound like a great, slow train. In daylight, San Francisco is monochromatic across the bay, soft as chalk, close but unreal.

Commercially, Bridge Way is mostly shoppes and restaurants: one bright little boutique after another, like Carmel's Ocean Street, but closer together and quicker-paced; a faint, strange feeling of New York sometimes, and autumn, though I can't imagine why that should be. The general tone of the shoppes this year has been hippie, but modishly, expensively so. This is especially interesting when you consider that Sausalito, taken flower child for flower child, has the stringiest, most depressing lot of hippies dragging around

Artist Jean Varda's boat, Sausalito

that I've seen anywhere. It's hard to explain the amazing falling-off in quality, but they often turn out to be refugees from the Haight-Ashbury, unable to get behind that scene either. They wore the earth bare in the pretty plaza off Bridge Way this year, sitting around.

On the other hand, as a town for looking at girls, Sausalito is unsurpassed in my knowledge of California. The great majority of them undoubtedly come shopping and sporting from San Francisco, Berkeley, and all over the Bay Area and Marin, but they're far more visible here, on crowded, narrow Bridge Way, than they would likely be at home. It's a matter of distribution, concentration, proportion — setting, if you will. Fifth Avenue used to have something of this quality at lunchtime, when all the secretaries come out; but the New York clogged-pore dinginess was at work even on the prettiest of them, eating at their bones and eyes. They never looked quite healthy.

But, oh my, the girls in Sausalito. They come at you like punches — combinations, one to the stomach, two quick hard ones to the imagination, another in the stomach, one wicked belt to the heart — or like anti-aircraft fire bursting all around you. I think of that image because during the war, on my block at least, we believed that the Japanese Zeros were so flimsily made that even the concussion of a shell exploding nearby would knock them out of the air. That's what I feel like on Bridge Way sometimes, a Zero.

It's the California look, the California clothes, the California way of standing flat-footed with the head half-turned, so that the tan throat shows full and tight as a sail, and the cheekbone repeating the expectancy of the jugular vein. I don't mean California as a state or a civilization when I write this, but California as an idea of America: warm and tall and lucky, with plenty of vaccines and orange juice, innocent, terrible, beautiful, all in a way that has never been before. When I was in Europe, I could never understand why my friends were so utterly preoccupied with American girls, beyond beauty, beyond money, beyond comparative ease of seduction. I think I do, now. They made fun of those girls, waiting to pick them up after class at the Alliance Française, but they warmed their hands at them somehow. Me, New Yorker, I liked the European girls, the ones who knew what winter was. I didn't dig the California chicks at all.

On weekends nights along Bridge Way, the cars seem to be backed up all the way to Lombard Street in San Francisco. Their headlights look pale and fuzzy, because of the dampness in the air, but their tops reflect the streetlights and the bright doorways. The Glad Hand is red; Ondine's is a tremulous blue-white; the window of the Tides Bookshop is gaslamp yellow. But the street is full of a shifting phosphorescence, unaccountable to any one source — like the music — unless Sausalito is gently giving back the hard, far light of San Francisco. People spill through that odd aurora, lovely and frantic as moths, but on such nights I can never understand a word that anyone is saying. The whole street begins to rock slowly and strongly after a while, with the swing of the raddled black-silk bay. Late at night, the water lightens in color to the blue-gray of airmail paper.

Yet I become restless in Sausalito after a few days. It would be good to live here as Mike does: private by the water, working, involved with the community of artists and people who like art — pleasantly tangled up with Sausalito. But it's a thin, unsatisfying town to visit, unless you're a sailing nut, or a shopping nut, or an eating nut. The best thing about Sausalito, finally, is that it is the gateway to Marin County. And Marin — in keeping with my California wariness of loving places that many people love, I would very much have liked not to care about Marin. But I couldn't manage it, and the only person I know who might have is Mark Twain's owl, the one who was a good deal disappointed about Yo Semite. Oh boy, Marin.

Mill Valley, Corte Madera, Inverness, Tomales, Point Reyes Station, Bolinas. I'm still unsure about Marin geography, and towns skate slowly around in my mind, like a mobile; but it contents me to say those names. The peninsula is all hills, crumpled as though they been squeezed up between giant knuckles. It's no good for farming, but dairy and beef cattle have thrived here since Mexican times. Canyons are deep, and the roads are narrow, so you're always coming over and around and being taken by surprise. Except for the coast, it's nowhere truly spectacular, and yet I continually hear myself saying, "Oh. Oh, *look* at that." There is a kind of beauty that comforts, and that's Marin.

Muir Woods, in Redwood Creek canyon below Mount Tamalpais, is a good, dark place that always feels quiet, no matter how crowded it may be. Perhaps because of its smallness (504 acres), it's immediately comprehensible in a way that the great national parks aren't. This is it, this is what we have lost: not even so much the trees and the wild things and the sound of water, but the quiet darkness. I'm sour about my other places being invaded by shrillness and candy wrappers, but I'd never grudge anyone Muir Woods. I think it should be requisite for people who work in the county, who sell or study, work at San Quentin or Hamilton Air Force Base or put up tract homes, to spend some part of each day in Muir Woods. It wouldn't be mandatory for it to make a difference.

Mount Tamalpais itself is more like a small ridge with three summits. You can do practically anything here — picnic, camp out, hike, sort of ski, fly kites, roll downhill, lie in the grass with girls, lie in the grass with children, savor the lupine and the sky,

Sausalito houseboats

Sausalito waterfront

sleep and wake. There's a huge natural amphitheatre on the west slope of the mountain where you can sit on terraced stone seats — or climb higher and wriggle out a place between the madrone root — and watch plays and concerts. The light is nice here, warm and coarse.

I'm sure the Point Reyes peninsula can't really be my favorite part of Marin County. That would be absurd, because I hate the cold, and Point Reyes has the usual northern Pacific shore climate. Scenically, the area has been badly short-changed on the Marin feeling of richness, and the San Andreas Fault heightens the peculiar sense of isolation by almost severing Point Reyes from the mainland. I've only been here once, with Mike — we bicycled across the peninsula and picnicked on the beach. Yet I have dreamed about Point Reyes a couple of times since then, and I have no idea why.

There's a meadow, I remember — an unbelievably wide and brilliant meadow with deer. The paths that lead to the beach are closed in and canopied by alders and laurel until you come to a place where flowered bluffs fly out on either hand, and the sea wind begins. You have to bicycle another half-mile on a thin, white, rutted road, and then you leave the bike and walk down the bluff to the beach, through nameless green and gold higher than your head.

The girl who came with us was walking back through a day she had spent at Point Reyes with her lover. He was going away, and she wanted to give him the day to take with him in photographs. Mike took pictures of her as she ran, laughed, picked ferns, smoked, sat still — doing everything alone that they had done together. Even the lunch she packed for the three of us to eat on the beach was a re-enactment of the meal she had brought along that day. Maybe that's why I dreamed about Point Reyes, and still remember it as beautiful and strange. I felt a little like a ghost, and ghost watch things very closely.

The bulk of the Marin County population is concentrated in the southern end of the peninsula, in cities like San Rafael, San Anselmo, and Mill Valley, because of its nearness to San Francisco, and because of the milder weather. But the north country, up along the Inverness Ridge and shallow, brown Tomales Bay, is equally as lovely in a different way. Colors are sharper and more sudden than they are further south, and you can see farther. It's a mixture of highland wildness and New England coves, mudflats, and oyster beds. The villages are small, surviving mostly off dairy products; the white clapboards and red roofs shade into gray and smoky blue near the water. It feels secret, though no place in Marin really is any more.

Up at Marshall, in a former resort hotel overlooking Tomales Bay, a Synanon House has been established for the last couple of years. In the Random House International Dictionary, published in 1966, Synanon is defined as *a private organization assisting those who wish to be cured of narcotics addiction.* But Chester Stern, secretary-treasurer of the Synanon Foundation, has declared, "By the end of 1967, the editors at Random House will have to change this definition, for Synanon will be a word, a place, an idea and an attitude toward life familiar to millions of the world's citizens." Between the first definition and the second, there is a significant tension.

Synanon originated in 1958 in Ocean Park, California, when a forty-three-year-old ex-alcoholic named Chuck Dederich began using his beach flat as a center for weekly discussions among a few alcoholics and dope addicts. The flat quickly became both the sanctuary and the emotional hub of a growing group, many of whom moved into nearby apartments to be close to Dederich and to one another. That summer, Dederich rented a larger storefront building and incorporated Synanon as a non-profit organization. The names comes from an illiterate addicts jumbling of the words *seminar* and *symposium*.

(Synanon's publicity, from the beginning, has been a fascinating blend of sophisticated Madison Avenue techniques and classical religious propaganda. In either case, the idea is to be remembered; and remembered in someone else's words. The history of Synanon has a Biblical cadence, full of sacred mnemonics: from the fact that Chuck Dederich's unemployment check in Ocean Park was $33 a week, to the clash between the alcoholics and the addicts, and the break with A.A.; the move to Santa Monica, and the hearings before the frightened, antagonistic City Council there; the night of "the Big Cop-out" on July 20, 1959, when the addicts living at Synanon made their commitment to a drugless way of life. Words and phrases are stylized — an addict is always a "dope fiend," and a "child," and his behavior is "stupid." One who leaves Synanon without "graduating" is a "splitee"; while a person who becomes a success is rewarded with status and responsibility, and held up as a "role-model." You get the feeling sometime that everyone at Synanon talks the same way, which isn't true.)

Synanon's technique — and there can be very little doubt by now that Dederich's methods do work, at least with certain types of addicts — is grounded on two absolutes: first, that a drug user is a weak, defeated personality, "addicted to stupidity," in the Synanon phrase; and, secondly, that only another addict can help him change his life. From the moment he enters Synanon (to be immediately cut off from narcotics and, traditionally, kick his habit on a cot or a couch, in public) he will be put down, derided, exposed, goaded, shamed, and occasionally patted on the back — but always by people who have been exactly where he is. No longer reinforced by a surrounding society of self-pitying equals, he will be treated like a little boy until he becomes angry enough to prove that he isn't one. The other two alternatives, both still in force, have been to treat him either as a criminal or as a patient. Neither one has worked.

Angelo DiLucca is twenty-six, and has been at Synanon for a year and a half, first in Santa Monica, and then in Marshall. (There are four other Synanon facilities, located in San Francisco, San Diego, New York, and Detroit; though only the California establishments actually house addicts.) Angelo is from Brooklyn; instantly familiar — the sort of cheerfully menacing Italian punk who used to bust up our punchball games and take over the field. He has been the route: an addict and a thief exactly half his life, in and out of Elmira and Leavenworth; an old hand at kicking narcotics for the duration, or to pare an expensive habit down to a manageable size, but without any motivation to stay clean. Today he looks clean in both senses of the word — absolutely scrubbed and shining, bouncing with energy. Like most of the Synanon people you meet, he is easily friendly, and eager to talk about his past life, and his new world.

"Man, I was nothing, and I thought I was something. You know, no matter how bad it got — how much I had to steal, the things I had to do — man, I was cool. I knew I was cool. I was just like out of the world, and all the things they did to me, put me in jail, give me pills, tests, long talks about my old man — well, that was all happening in the world, it didn't mean nothing to me. And picture — I was starving. I mean, I was starving. I weighed a hundred and eight pounds when I went to Santa Monica. I was really dying, Pete. I'd be dead by now if it wasn't for Synanon."

The easiest part is getting off drugs, he says. Anybody can do it; movies and legends have made withdrawal seem a lot more harrowing than it generally is. "The real hard thing is learning that you got to start all over. Chuck gave me a talk the first day — he said, look, you're not a man, you're a twenty-five-year-old baby. A baby. You haven't learned a damn thing all the time you've been alive. Now you got to grow up, or you'll die. Man, he made me mad! I stayed mad a long time, too. Got my head shaved two times." Head-shaving is one of three standard punishments at Synanon. The other two are loss of privileges, and expulsion.

Angelo is an important person in the Tomales Bay facility now. Beginning as all new residents do — washing dishes, scrubbing floors, and scouring latrines — he has worked his way into the position of commissary chief: in charge not only of the kitchen, but of hustling food for the community, which means going into San Francisco at least once a week. He laughs whenever he talks about his job. "I don't know *anything* about running a kitchen, I mean it. I'm just sort of making things up as I go along. That's what everybody does here. That's the way Synanon is."

In the San Francisco Synanon House — a converted warehouse known as the Seawall — John Minervino Rodriguez is still cleaning latrines, having only been here for a few months. But he already shares one very significant privilege with Angelo DiLucca: that of mixing with the visitors who come to the regular Saturday-night open houses at the Seawall. As he says himself, "You have to want to do this, and they have to choose you. Maybe the director says you aren't ready yet. And if you don't get out and be with the people, like I'm talking to you now, then they might take you right off the floor. I like it, I dont't mind. I like to talk to people."

John is from Ponce, Puerto Rico, but he grew up in the South Bronx, around 149th Street. He began using narcotics at fourteen; he is twenty-two now. Brown-skinned, handsome, with a look of baby-fatness still remaining, he talks about his past with less humor than Angelo, and with a kind of wonder. "I was a thief. I stole from everybody, from my own family. My aunt, my cousins, they would come to see my mother, and they maybe put their bags down in the bedroom, you know, and I'd be right in there, so fast, oh boy. My mother, she knew what I did, she knew I was strung out, but she didn't say nothing. She would give back the money, if she could, but she didn't say nothing to anybody. You know, she didn't know what to do. She didn't speak English, she didn't know what to do."

Told that he looks very happy, he smiles and turns his hand palm up on the table. "I am happy. I never was happy in my whole life. Of course, I got a long, long way to go yet, but I'm working hard. They're gonna put me on at the gas station next month — that's a real good job. You can get any job you want here, if you work hard enough. What I really want is, I want to get to be a Wizard. Only you have to know about everything to be a Wizard, and you have to be real good in the games. I'm not so good in the games yet."

The Game; the Wizard. These are two of the basic concepts invented at Synanon as tools to use in breaking down the defenses and self-justifications of what Chuck Dederich calls "the addictive personality." In a Synanon Game, a selected group of eight to twelve people, one of whom will be a "synanist" — guide and player at the same time — will sit in a room for several hours, alternately attacking one another's rationalizations for their recent behavior, and desperately defending their own. It is a brutal, merciless session, in which no kind of violence except the physical is barred. Being good at the Game involves what Tom Patton of the Tomales Bay House has called ". . . the spirit of ancient oriental archery where the defender is never vanquished and the attacker aims at himself."

San Francisco from Marin County

At Synanon, the power structure is deliberately paternal and pyramidal, with no room at all for rebellion; but in the Game all badges of rank are off, and all smoldering resentments and grievances are laid out. Anything can be said to anyone, and very little can be hidden for long. Residents of Synanon, with rare exceptions, play the Game three times a week. I've never met anyone there who wasn't completely committed to it.

"You learn something about yourself every minute," Angelo says. "Even if you're not the one getting worked over. Like once there was this kid working in the commissary with me, and Jesus, he was giving me a hard time. You couldn't trust him with nothing. He was dumb, all right, but he wasn't as dumb as he made out to be. So I said to myself, okey, I'm really gonna get this jerk in the Game tonight. But somebody else jumped him before I did, and all of a sudden I got to thinking, 'Well, you dumb sonofabitch, how come you always pick lames like him to work with you?' Always, like back when I was ten years old, I always used to have one big, dumb buddy messing things up, so I'd look good and nothing was ever my fault. Now remember, I suddenly figured all this out in maybe five seconds, and then I started defending him like crazy. They all ganged me then, but that was okay. But that's the way you find things out in the Game, when it's all happening so fast."

"It's not a game," the green-eyed girl at the Seawall says very quietly. "They call it a game, but now it's as much a part of my life as eating or sleeping. You don't feel that way about a game."

Her name is Gail, and she lives and works at the San Francisco Synanon House, but she has never been a dope addict, or even taken a sleeping pill. She got involved with Synanon through the Game Clubs — the "square Games." Outsiders, non-addicts, middle-class squares have been playing the Game under the guidance of Synanon personnel since 1960; and there has been a lengthening waiting list of applicants since 1964, when Synanon came to San Francisco. The Game Clubs became official in 1966, and Synanon now claims over a thousand dues-paying members in San Francisco, San Diego, Santa Monica, Reno, and New York. This is slightly more than the total number of Synanon residents.

Again, I've never met a square who wasn't enthusiastic about the Game Clubs. Nobody who was less than enthusiastic would be likely to keep playing the Game. Few of them have moved into a Synanon House, like Gail (though Synanon's plans for the near future include a growing non-addict population), but what she says of the Game is what the others say. "It has changed me. Psychiatry doesn't change anything, because even if you manage to make yourself be pretty honest with your psychiatrist, it's still just that one person, that one room, that hour on Tuesday and Friday. But the Game reaches into your life, it won't stay separate. You find that you just can't be honest in the Game and a liar the rest of the time. It doesn't work, you can't function. So you learn to function in the rest of the world as you do in the Game. I don't know any other therapy — religion, philosophy, whatever — that has that effect on you."

Asked if the atmosphere at Synanon couldn't be considered a hiding place, a comforting

PHILIP HYDE. *Ano Nuevo Island, Santa Cruz County Coast*

MICHAEL BRY. *Bode, Mono County*

MICHAEL BRY. *Mendocino*

MICHAEL BRY. *Tinsley Island, Sacramento River delta country*

PHILIP HYDE. *Jedediah Smith Redwood Park, Del Norte County*

MICHAEL BRY. *Pebble Beach*

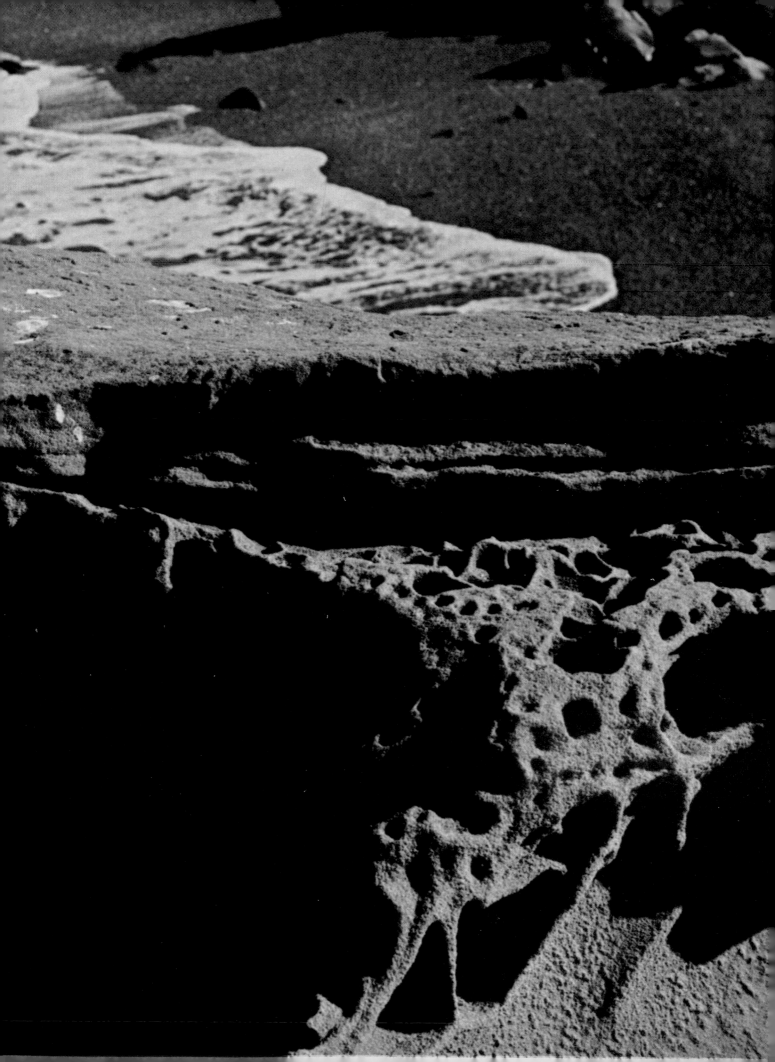

JOHN WAGGAMAN. *Salk Institute for Biological Studies, La Jolla*

MICHAEL BRY. *View from Sentinel Dome, Yosemite Park*

womb, she replies gently, "I've never felt as exposed and unprotected as I do here. I've been hiding all my life."

But a friend, a graduate student in criminology at Berkeley, who has attended a number of square Games, says angrily, "Those things are just cruel, vulgar exercises in self-disgust and self-indulgence. As far as curing drug addiction goes, Synanon's done better than any other outfit — I'll give them that gladly. But their man Dederich has this absolute dogma that all forms of addiction are fundamentally the same; that shooting heroin is the same thing as being a homosexual, or being promiscuous, or a compulsive eater, or speeding. Well, it isn't — it just isn't so. They're coming on more and more like a messianic religious movement, sucking in a lot of the bored, confused, unhappy middle-class people who are always drawn to authoritarian groups like Synanon. I'm sorry about it. I used to have a great deal of respect for Synanon, and I still admire what they've done for drug addicts. But I don't respect them any more."

In ten years Synanon has come an astonishingly long way from the flat in Ocean Park. The organization owns a considerable amount of land; it operates service stations and industrial plants; it has exclusive distribution rights to a number of handcrafted products; and it raises large amounts of cash and other gifts both from foundations and from individual sponsors. (The people I walked with in San Francisco and Marshall insist that Synanon has no fixed entrance fee, and that no addict is ever turned away for lack of money. But several Synanon publications mention that the families of addicts are "encouraged to contribute from $500 to $1000," to insure their interest in Synanon; and Peter Collier, writing in *Ramparts*, cites evidence that poorer applicants have in fact been rejected.) An excellent school for the children of residents has been established at the Marshall facility. Synanon members are instructing inmates of the Nevada State Penitentiary in the use of Synanon techniques, at the invitation of the state; and the basic method is steadily being adopted by private and federal institutions from Staten Island to Mendocino County.

Synanon is decidedly hostile to most of its imitators: specifically the ones who employ its methods with the limited aim of treating drug addiction. You can't talk for long to a staff member without hearing a restatement of Chuck Dederick's belief that addicts happen to be cured at Synanon as a "side-effect" of living in the Synanon community, playing the Game, and becoming a responsible citizen. In the last year or two, there has been noticeably less talk about sending graduates back into society, and much more about expansion, about the new concept of apartment "clumps" and Synanon cities, populated to a large degree by squares. Such alliances as Synanon makes these days are with organizations that stress the search for new forms of community, and the need for changed relationships between human beings. Esalen Institute, down at the Big Sur Hot Springs, is probably the best example of such a group. Dederich frequently speaks there, and they play a variant of the Synanon Game.

13. "Here I Am in the Promised Land, and I Don't Like It."

(BIG SUR AND ESALEN)

I once hitched a ride with a young couple who were on their way to visit a friend in a Santa Cruz hospital. She had undergone a nervous breakdown a few days before; on her own, as they were quick to point out — that is, it wasn't the result of a bad LSD trip, but an old-fashioned, self-propelled crackup. "She had this transcendental experience in a Greyhound terminal," the girl explained. "It suddenly came over her that this was the place to practice some of the techniques she'd been learning at Esalen. Body awareness — you know about Esalen? Well, the people in the bus station thought she was a nympho-maniac. People are very uptight in bus stations."

That remains my basic image of Esalen Institute, and it certainly isn't a fair one. A great many remarkable people have been involved with Esalen since its founding in 1962 — S. I. Hayakawa, Arnold Toynbee, Alan Watts, Bishop James A. Pike, Carl Rogers, B. F. Skinner, Ray Bradbury, Abraham Maslow, Fritz Perls, Buckminster Fuller, George B. Leonard, Ali Akbar Khan — and the New York *Times* estimates that "some 100,000 Californians have participated in at least one of the movement's activities, which are devoted to the cultivation of feelings." Nothing wrong with that — who can be against the cultivation of feelings? The fact is that people are very uptight in bus stations.

They're very uptight in a lot of other places too, but you observe it more readily in bus stations; just as it's much easier to sense the inescapable insanity of cold, dirty New York than it is to catch the madness of California, where the weather and the manners are generally better. In New York you obviously have to be mad to survive, but the great lure of California to an Easterner is the idea that here there may be an alternative to madness. Possibly a couple of alternatives.

It's been a truism for a long time that the important currents in this country are flowing from west to east; that whatever is happening — or simply becoming visible at last — in California this year will be happening in New York next year, and that, like patterns of magnetic force, the connections will be crackling out across the mysterious land between these two poles, passing through the air and the earth with equal ease. In practice, this is generally taken to mean that boys in Steubenville, Ohio, are walking around lugging surfboards under their arms, and that the girls in Scotland, South Dakota, are suddenly

Big Sur

all painting butterflies on their knees. For me, it's epitomized in the idea of student demonstrations taking place at the University of Pittsburgh. When I was there, during Eisenhower's second term, the student body would never have believed that it had a right to become angry about the testing of hydrogen bombs on the campus. Now even the fraternities open their meetings by singing "*We Shall Overcome*," and close with Bob Dylan's song about Mr. Jones. So I'm told, anyway.

But California's most significant influences during the coming years are likely to concern the pursuit of happiness. I can't prove it statistically, but I'm quite sure that California, proportionately speaking, has a larger number of unhappy people who *know* they're unhappy, and think about it a lot, than any other state. It has a lot to do with having the time to consider unhappiness, and the money to try to relieve it — the "increased leisure" and "higher standard of living" that has been the American idea of happily-ever-after for so long. Hence Esalen, at Big Sur, and in Steubenville and Scotland, South Dakota, in time.

My generation may yet go down as the one that knew what was wrong with it. The popularization of psychiatric catch-phrases and catch-concepts, the rapidity of their diffusion, and the geometrically increasing self-consciousness of the American individual (and this cuts across all races and classes, though it manifests itself in drastically different ways) all combine to produce a unique level of public awareness of discontent and frustration; as well as a fantastic kind of public articulateness. Surely no nation, no civilization, has ever studied itself and talked about itself as much as this one. We walk around *tripes au soleil*, guts in the sun, taking the idea that the unexamined life is not worth living as a guarantee of the examined life.

"Here I am in the Promised Land, and I don't like it. I don't not like it, either. I don't know what I really feel about anything. The job's good, and sometimes it gets interesting, and I'm doing all right, but it's just a job. I feel like I'm faking it all the time, like everyone else is grown up and I'm not, and I'd better not let them find out. I can't talk to her. I know it bothers her that I don't touch her enough, but I never really could touch anybody, unless I'd been drinking. I like it when the kids touch me, but they just come and go. I could talk to them if they'd just sit down a minute. I'm overweight. I drink too much. I watch TV too damn much, and I know it's lousy, but I don't care. I wish I cared. There's nothing I want, but I'm lonely. I'm lonely. I can't talk to anybody, except maybe Charley, and not Charley so much any more. Jesus Christ, is it going to be like this for the rest of my life? Is this it?"

Admittedly, this is white-middle-class malaise expressing itself: fat, ugly, self-pitying, and as totally irrelevant to the suffering of a Bolivian peasant as though it were uttered by a Martian. But these are people too, and their sorrows and hungers and suicides are no less painful and important for being undignified. The American middle class makes the world, and what haunts it today will be bothering the Cubans and Chinese tomorrow, and the Bolivians the day after — next week, anyway, if there is a next week. Revolutionaries — like Luis Valdez in Delano — want their people to have the material goods of the fat Americans without acquiring the grotesque hangups and the fears. I don't know if it's possible. There's a girl in Romain Gary's novel, *The Ski Bum*, who prays not to find out that Negroes really are just like everyone else, no worse and no better.

In a sunny room at Esalen, I watch a television tape of one of Fritz Perls's gestalt-therapy sessions. His groups meet in this same room, sitting in a circle under the eye of a TV camera. Whoever volunteers to be the subject of a session takes the chair next to Fritz Perls, and the camera focuses solely on her as she talks about herself. The tape can be instantaneously replayed, which is a gimmick that everybody's having fun with right now. Americans are fascinated with the idea of watching themselves, and of watching themselves watch themselves. It's supposed to add an extra dimension to the Synanon Game, to happenings and light shows, and to other sorts of group therapy; especially when the tape is played back while the action it records is still going on. The older I get, the better I understand why certain primitive tribes absolutely refuse to let themselves be painted or photographed.

The woman is in her late thirties or early forties: well-dressed and not ugly, but with no slightest sense of enjoyed femaleness about her. She is crying and not crying by turns, as easily as one steps through dappled shadows on the path, but the tears never interrupt the flow of her talk. The tape seems to have begun in the middle of her soliloquy — for Fritz Perls hardly speaks, except to urge her gently along when she hesitates. It doesn't matter. She is talking, not about her dead mother, but to her.

"Mama, I never could tell you any of this. I always tried to talk to you, but you wouldn't let me. Just by being yourself, you wouldn't let me. I always became someone else when I talked to you, always, and everything I wanted to say got twisted up into whatever you wanted to hear. Mama, you don't know me, you never once saw me. I'm not at all the person I was with you. I'm different. I am somebody altogether different."

"Who are you?" Fritz Perls asks. The camera never leaves the woman's soft, crumpled face.

"I'm Betty. *Mama, I'm Betty.* Betty is a real person, and she doesn't have to keep trying to please you. She can do the things that please her, the things that make her happy."

"Yes," says Fritz Perls. "And what makes Betty happy?"

She is silent for a moment, closing her eyes. "I don't know. I've never had the time to find out what Betty likes, what I might really enjoy doing, and be good at. I just go on, and go on, and once I tried kill myself. That was just to make Mama angry, I know that Fritz, and I won't try it again. I won't do anything to make you angry, Mama, or to make you happy, either." She laughs suddenly. "But I have to keep reminding Betty about that, because she forgets."

"What do you say to Betty, when she forgets?"

Again she laughs. "Oh, Fritz, I don't know, I can't." He says nothing, and she tightens her lips and shoves her uneasy hands down into her lap. "Well, I say: stop it. Do you hear me? Just stop it, don't be stupid. You can't do anything to make Mama like you any better. She's dead, she's dead, and it doesn't matter what she said to you or what she thought of you. And you can't blame Mama when you do stupid things, and you can't blame Mama if nobody likes you, and you can't blame Mama if you hate the job — " She is crying now, her face just sliding apart, melting, her fists beating on her thighs; her precise voice shredding, the way a sail will tear itself to pieces in a wind once the first rent has been forced, but never losing the articulateness. "You have to accept what you are, and learn to be glad of yourself — you can't keep saying Mama made me that way. You can't blame Mama any more."

It continues, to the end. There's no resolution, no special reason for it to be the end, but Fritz Perls finally stops her, mostly by making her laugh. The camera loosens its terrible grip on her, pulling back to show them together. He looks exactly as he ought to look (few people do, and it's a more serious problem than it sounds, in this age of instantaneous playbacks) — seventy-five years old, with a wild-bearded head like a mountain, and the stage presence of a natural actor. He clowns solemnly for Betty, insisting that she change roles with him. "Let me tell you my troubles, and you be me for a change. You know how to be me. Anybody can be wise old Fritz, it's much harder to be Betty." There is other laughter on the tape now, and I suddenly remember that ten or twelve people have been — had been — watching Betty as she tore away her own pitiful defenses and alibis. To be left with what? She says that she'd like to work with children someday. What else can Fritz Perls possibly do but make her laugh?

In the last minutes of the tape, Fritz is urged to address himself to Sigmund Freud, as though it were Freud in the chair next to him. Fritz Perls knew Freud in Vienna long ago, and his antagonism to Freudian methods of analysis is a standing joke among his own patients. The camera closes on Fritz's face, and he looks away into it with deep compassion.

"Sigmund Freud," he murmurs. "Sigmund Freud. A great mind, even a great understanding you are, *Doktor* Freud. But a sick man, a very sick man." Off-camera, the laughter grows again, but he does not seem to hear it. He goes on slowly, "So sure you are right — why will you never listen to anyone? I could help you, if you would listen to me. Because somehow, at the end of my life, I have fallen over this amazing secret that no one else seems to have noticed — that what is, *is*. . . ."

There's a story about a San Francisco reporter who challenged Fritz Perls during a seminar, saying, "I can't feel pain. Can you make me feel pain?" Fritz, who is still a strong man, walked around to his chair and hit him in the mouth. "Did you feel pain then?" he asked.

"No," said the reporter, "because I knew you were doing it for my own good. I didn't feel a thing."

They have other things at Esalen besides gestalt-therapy workshops. There are encounter groups playing the Synanon Game and its variants (the encounter-group technique is being steadily adopted by big corporations; most recently, the State Department), body

awareness classes, sensitivity training; seminars on meaningful coincidence, extra sensory perception, Kundalini Yoga, bioenergetic analysis, and sensory awakening for couples. Meditation is big, and dance therapy is even bigger. The various weekend workshops cost $60 to attend, while those lasting five days cost $155 to $175.

"I don't need anyone to tell me I have skin," Joan Baez says, speaking of Esalen and its purposes. But a girl named Marcia, a dancer who works with Esalen, tells me earnestly, "You can't imagine how many people don't know they're animals, living in animals' bodies. When I ask them to jump up and down, to roar, to roll over each other, to stamp on the ground — they really don't know how to do any of it. Well, they do know, but they've pushed their bodies so far away they can hardly move anymore. But when I get them doing it, stamping and screaming and dancing — wow, some of them go a little mad. Teachers, businessmen, advertising men. I wouldn't want to know who some of them are stamping on. They can't stop."

One of Esalen's most persistent quests is for an alternative to the one-dimensional relationship between teacher and pupil, artist and audience; he who pours and they who are filled full. Some time ago, an attempt was made to let those attending an Esalen-sponsored lecture in San Francisco express their opinions of what was being said at any given moment by flashing one of three colored cards to indicate, *Yes, go on, You're losing me,* or *Hey, I want to say something.* The lecture itself was reportedly a dull one, and people kept getting their cards confused, but the idea was good and important. Everything I write about Esalen seems to come out a little mocking, but they're asking the right questions. It's their sureness of finding the answers, and their readiness to mess with people that sometimes brings out the grump in me. One thing worth questioning in our times is the idea of answers.

The big answer just now is naturalness. Dropping your role, dropping labels and identities, putting the masks aside, relating to one another with nothing but the moment's honest emotions — naturalness has already developed its own recognizable jargon. Esalen recently inaugurated the "Psychomat" at Grace Cathedral, where some eighty strangers sat in groups discussing their feelings. Gerard Haigh, the Los Angeles psychologist who originated the Psychomat, talked about it to the newspapers afterward.

> *. . . One woman in my group looked sad. A young man noticed this and told her so. She admitted she was sad and began to cry. Another man said he wanted to hold her, so she cried while he held her.*
>
> *An older woman in the group immediately started conversation with someone else. When asked why she was doing it, she replied, "I feel embarrassed for her. I want to divert attention from her." In essence, she was telling the woman who was crying, "You are doing something wrong."*
>
> *The two women were beautiful examples of a conflict we all have. Society expects us to be mature, controlled adults who keep our cool — even when the little child in us wants to cry.*

Who can be against the cultivation of feelings? But it does remind me a little of the Brecht-Weill "*Alabama-Song*" ("We've lost our good old mamma, And must have whiskey, oh, you know why. . . ."); or of the commercial for the antacid made for that overstuffed feeling. *When you eat too well, demand Di-Gel!* American troubles. And yet, the pain is real.

I don't remember in which book Thomas Wolfe writes that Americans always believe that something can be done for them: that it's a matter of finding the right book, the right pill, the right place, the right courses, the right man, the right woman, the right cause. D. H. Lawrence says that America worships the human will, and it is true. We have no national sense of tragedy, no awe of the inevitable; and this lack has freed us to do many impossible things. But the price is heavy, and we pay it partly in the special kind of American victims we produce: the walking wounded who know desperately that they could be different if they made the right choice and practiced it faithfully every day. Even the idea of joyous acceptance — that what is, *is* — can only be presented and received as another hope of change. We have been diverting rivers, rooting up jungles, razing mountains, altering air and soil, bodies and minds and lives, far too long to begin going with the universe now. Our grandeur lies in this, and our terrible tragedy.

In the evening, Mike and I stand on the terrace of the lodge, talking with a Viennese lady of indeterminate age, as all Viennese ladies are. Actually, she's Polish, but she grew up in Vienna, and speaks with that accent. She is dressed all in pink — shoes, slacks, turtleneck blouse, nail polish — and even her hair has a quality of pink about it. Her face is lined, but she moves and looks at you with the slow assurance of attractiveness that Viennese ladies never lose.

This is a beautiful place, no question. There is a great stretch of slanting green meadow, with willows; and there are spidery wrought-iron railings, the kind you hardly ever see now. Left and right, the Big Sur hills come down like clamshells, and beyond the lawn the ragged cliffs and sea-canyons drop away. It is sunset: the sea is copper on the horizon, and then a strange, cold amber darkening in to shore. The Viennese lady sighs.

"I feel a little guilty always because I don't have a real reason to run up here from San Bernardino," she says. "Once I had a good excuse, because I was going to Fritz's workshops, but not for a long while now. I am very found of Fritz, and I learned something important from him, but I don't feel I need to go to him any more. I came this time to hear Alan Watts speak."

As the sun goes down, people seem to be moving unhurriedly to their positions. Soloists and choruses, cast as hippies or straights, or odd, in-between character parts; costumed in boots and serapes, in Empire and *belle-époque* gowns, in tweed sport coats and prim jumpers, in hostility, confusion, and gay gentleness, they find their proper places against the night sea. Some stand half in shadow under the willows; others walk slowly down the meadow and pause, etched in fire, while yet others walk on toward the sea, or lie down in the grass, or simply sit on railings, whistling pensively. I'd be slow to counsel people to give up the silhouettes they have wriggled into; the mask that has crusted over a wound. Sometimes it's the silhouette that is the living thing. It's not easy to tell.

"I don't really care if I hear Alan Watts or not," the Viennese lady says. "I just wanted to get away from San Bernardino. Why should you need an excuse to go off someplace where it's so pretty? Where you can go for walks?"

The Man-Made Environment

Ferndale House

The man on the left owns the trailer court and the mansion as well. He used to conduct tours through the house, but he doesn't any more. "Old man Ross brought the timber allawayroundtheHorn."

San Francisco, California Street

San Francisco Conservatory

Ox Cart at San Antonio de Padua Mission

Golden Gate Bridge

The Carson House in Eureka is claimed to be the most photographed residence in America—another of those California records. It was built in 1884 for William Carson, the lumber magnate. A good deal of his own redwood went into the construction, but hardly any of it is visible from the exterior. This is usually the case with redwood. I don't know why. "Lumber from the greatest lumber tree in the world is for the most part used hiddenly. From its magnificence in the living forest it goes to obscurity in man-made structures—in the ties that trains pass over, invisibly in the mines, in foundations that are not seen, time after time in supporting but concealed places. It is not possible to point out great or beautiful buildings and say they were made of redwood. This for nearly a century has been largely the fate of a wood which, without garniture, delights the gaze and never affronts it."

Alfred Powers
Redwood Country

Ferndale House

The famous gas-powered Skunk Train—and its recent addition, the diesel-fueled Superskunk—is one of those things that always fascinate me: the tourist attraction that continues to function at its original purpose. As it has done since the 1920's, the Skunk runs between Willits and Fort Bragg, along 40 miles of contorted narrow-gauge track (that may wriggle 8½ miles to cover an actual distance of 1½ miles), through a damp jungle of redwoods and summer camps. There is no other practical transportation in the area, and the Skunk carries everything that goes in or out— hunters, campers, mail, supplies, lumber. It's run for children as much as anything these days, with a stewardess and a clowning conductor named K. O. Nelson (he gives out cards); but it still works, too, which is nice.

A lumber mill in Trinity County. The booms and surges of the California economy since World War II haven't really touched the Northwest, except to drain away population. The marketable timber is running out fast, and tourism certainly hasn't made up for it. Things may change when the new dams and power plants are completed, when a couple of big roads are finally put through, and when the tourists start to spill out of the Sierra Nevada. I like the country just the way it is, but I don't live here.

Near Mono Lake. I think these cars must have made it to California out of the Dust Bowl, thirty years ago.

Just below the new Oroville Dam. Much of this area may have been flooded by the time this book is published.

The existence of the Fresno Mall is a great deal more significant than the fact that it feels a bit like Disneyland. Fresno itself is a typically ugly California city — typical in the sense that it blew up mindlessly from a little San Joaquin Valley town, laid out in a grid along the railroad track, into a miniature Los Angeles, complete with smog, sprawl, and troubles. Many cities in California have that look, as though some very important time between littleness and hugeness had simply been skipped. Eastern towns are ugly too, but each is bad in its own way, out of its own heavy history. The uniform, interchangeable ugliness of most large California cities is uniquely saddening because you can see so clearly that they didn't have to be like that.

Anyway, Fresno — of all cities — has built the first downtown shopping mall in California. They fought like hell for it, too. San Francisco might have built a hipper one, but San Francisco is busy with subways and second decks for the Golden Gate Bridge. Good for Fresno.

If California could ever conquer its traditional mania for the quick buck, it might make a very nice future, instead of just the future.

Disneyland

14. Well, the Children Will Have a Good Time

(DISNEYLAND, LOS ANGELES AND AS FOR SAN FRANCISCO . . .)

One brief reflection on Disneyland, although everything that can be said about that Forest Lawn of fancy, that lime pit of the imagination, has been said. I have a passionately sincere hatred for Walt Disney that usually burns away coldly inside me, but now and then blazes into helpless, sputtering hysteria. I think that man was the devil — the endless Enemy of everybody who ever made up a story; of every child who ever knew a story by heart, and corrected his mother if she changed a word, all the while thinking about the way it must really have been. Pausing at this point, I remember what he did to T. H. White's masterpiece, *The Sword in the Stone*, and that old strangling fury has me again. How dare he? How dare he? The Disney version of *The Jungle Book* will be in town in a few weeks. My children will want to go, and they'll love it. Good. I'm glad they're not cranks like me. Happy-go-lucky Baloo; white-skinned Mowgli; and a new character, an ape called "King Louis," whose voice is Louis Prima. I hate Walt Disney.

But about Disneyland. (My God, hasn't anybody ever thought about that name for an hour or so? Disneyland — last known residence of Alice, Cinderella, Huck Finn, Abraham Lincoln, and New Orleans jazz. Even the guy at Forest Lawn didn't call it "Eatonville.") There are two really good pitches, both located on the 1890s-ish Main Street. The first is a penny arcade with a fine collection of slot machines and shooting galleries. Since childhood, I have been incapable of passing one of those places, or of leaving one with a coin in my pocket; and I take my electric ratings of Sheriff, Ace, and Bombardier very seriously. Not to mention my score with the Grip-O-Meter, or my skill in holding a racing car on a road that keeps sliding away from me. I'm deadly with these things, this penny world.

The other good place is a drugstore, supposed to duplicate the small-town pharmacies of not all that long ago. It does, too. It smells right, and they have the right candies and lozenges in tall, dim glass jars, and even the dark give of the floor under your feet is just right. If it weren't for the Upjohn advertising all over the place, it would be something more than perfect — almost scary, almost free. But that's the tipoff, the curious clumsiness that keeps money on your mind every moment in Disneyland. I don't think he — they, now; It — could have helped it, even had he been aware of it, and wanted to. Being the devil has certain practical advantages, but there's that one lame, cloven foot, always.

For the rest of it — the Mississippi sidewheeler, Tom Sawyer's Island, the funicular ride up the plastic Matterhorn, the speech by Mr. Lincoln, the pirate cove, the journey on the jungle river, the costumed merchants and the storybook characters strolling around — well, the children will have a great time. Children can have a great time anywhere. I guess what I object to is the implicit statement that all this belongs to Walt Disney; that it exists nowhere else but in the official Disney version, in the toys and games and records, in the new storybooks manufactured from the screenplays. The worst thing is that in time it will be true. As redwood trees and lions and blue whales become extinct, their incredibly detailed and lifelike replicas will appear in Disney's pale kingdom, and nowhere else.

All right, I loved Donald Duck too. No ordinary, spiritless hack can get to be the devil. It takes hard work, and total dedication, and talent.

"The only way to write about Los Angeles," Marshall Lumsden says, "is to think of yourself as traveling in a foreign country. Liechtenstein, Luxembourg. You look up your expatriate friends, and any natives you met when they were visiting America, and you find a good place to get your dollars changed. And you keep a journal." He looks out of his office window in the Times-Mirror Building, and adds, "This country doesn't really have any natives, though. Even if you've spent your whole life in Los Angeles, you're not a native, not the way Liechtenstein has natives. The place keeps changing out from under you. You can't be a native of a temporary country. Not the way we're used to the word, anyway."

My attitude towards Los Angeles has always been that of the San Franciscan: a shifting mixture of contempt and fear. Politically, the soul of Los Angeles is represented in loving, hip, free San Francisco — where Proposition 14, the anti-open-housing bill of 1964, passed by a 2-1 margin, as it did everywhere else — by Sam Yorty, by Max Rafferty, by the most savage cops west of Ruleville, Mississippi, by Ronald Reagan. Culturally, of course, the place is Dallas with surfers. Its folk art is Disneyland; the high point of its Renaissance is Forest Lawn; its modern Medicis are the Chandler family and Sears Roebuck, for whom Vincent Price buys paintings. Money They have, far more than deserving We, but taste and understanding are eternally denied them by the mysterious will of God. It's all hustlers and hucksters down there — realtors, oil men, movie men, religious maniacs, insurance salesmen. What sensitive person would live in Los Angeles, when he could be walking with his baby down by the San Francisco Bay, providing he could find a parking place? Anybody who does live in Los Angeles, therefore . . .

There's a French book about Italy whose title alone epitomizes this view. It's called *Pour Italie*, meaning "As for Italy . . ." which is the way the French always begin to put down the Italians — their third favorite target, after Americans and Belgians. I mention this because Paris and San Francisco have been promulgating the same myth about themselves for a long time: the myth that they have taste, that they are the custodians of civiliza-

tion in their respective countries. I believed that once, easily, the way you believe that your beloved has brains.

Leaving Paris out of it (though places that hold Jerry Lewis retrospectives shouldn't throw stones), the fact is that Los Angeles has every tangible Good Thing that San Francisco has, and usually more of it. The museums are better; the theatre is much more varied and interesting — it wasn't Los Angeles that let the Actors Workshop die, and it wasn't San Francisco that staged *The Amen Corner* and *Catch My Soul* — and the new buildings are at least no worse. There are fewer good restaurants in Los Angeles, granted, but the good ones are very good; and the jazz scene is better now, though that's a very recent development. When I came west, eight years ago, San Francisco owned jazz, all of it, and rented it out to other cities from time to time. Today San Francisco doesn't care about jazz or jazz musicians, but only about the image of itself as Jazz City. San Francisco is bored with everything but its image, while Los Angeles is still crude enough to care about art as something real. The trouble over Michael McClure's play *The Beard* — police raids, actors arrested, injunctions and counter-injunctions, and the play going defiantly on — points this up, curiously enough, like the riots in Dublin at O'Casey plays. Los Angeles pays art the compliment of assuming it to be dangerous and powerful. San Francisco knows better.

As for the Bad Things, the unique horrors of the Los Angeles life-style, there are none that San Francisco doesn't share. The Bay city's freeways are choked and ugly; its black ghetto is as damning as Watts, and as inflammable; it came within an ace of putting a freeway through Golden Gate Park, and it will fill the Bay with garbage in my lifetime, and build on it; and that stuff in the air hasn't been just fog for some time now. Urban sprawl? Los Angeles is indeed spilling up the coast to Santa Barbara, and south to San Diego; but San Francisco sits smugly on its hills entirely surrounded by things like Pacifica, South San Francisco, and Daly City, the town that inspired *Little Boxes*. Realtor amusements, Rotarian popular culture? San Francisco did give birth to the best of the new rock bands (though The Doors are a Los Angeles group), but it is more likely to be remembered for topless dancers with poisoned, custardy breasts, and — by me, at least — for the Girl In The Cage: the one who grins and struts and sings silently, hour after hour, high over Broadway just before you hit the Bayshore Freeway. You can't defend San Francisco by arguing specific points, not any more. Around midnight, or even earlier, you have to fall back on mystique.

And there you do have the edge, the edge that only Raymond Chandler could have debated with any heart, and only before the war. For San Francisco is the Mystique Capital of the World, to give it its proper California designation; and Los Angeles has been short of the stuff from the beginning, as it has always lacked water. But you can't divert fairy tales, or irrigate with legends; no aqueduct will ever carry south whatever it is that makes people write bad songs about San Francisco. It's nothing San Francisco has ever earned, or wouldn't sell cheerfully if it could be isolated — it's just there, due to circumstances beyond our control. Setting is most of it, probably, but not all. We can sell the setting, and we will, but that other will hang around the sleek new ruins somehow, having nowhere else to go.

The New Yorker ran a cartoon recently that depicted a motorist's journey from Northern to Southern California: beginning among green fields populated by nymphs, centaurs, and piping satyrs, and progressing slowly into a bulldozed land of tract homes, patio barbecues, drive-ins, and signs reading IMPEACH EARL WARREN. It's true, but it isn't *that* true, I know it, but I still believe the cartoon. Such is the power of a good, solid mystique.

But the final edge is on Los Angeles's sword, really, because mystique is obsolete, as far as cities go, and so is the City that San Francisco exemplifies. Los Angles is the future: not a city at all, but a region — a country, as Marshall Lumsden says — many-centered, without sidewalks, held loosely together by freeways that connect one desire with another. The idea of walking a city, or knowing it, of living in it instead of only using it, of feeling something for it, love or hate — this is dying, as surely as feudalism died; and it is both fascinating and frightening to watch, as the other death must have been. Los Angeles is the future; and San Francisco will slump mumbling into senility — or burn to the ground — believing to the end that simply being San Francisco will pay its way forever. It will, too, right up to the end.

Los Angeles is the future; but I'll always remember an evening I spent with Mike down among the big white floating buildings of the new Civic Center there. The fountains were going, and the colored lights — *shah*, Tennessee Williams — and it was all beautiful and glowing, but there was no picture. Mike stomped around talking to himself, trying to find an angle with some teeth in it, and I trailed after him, lugging the tripod. We hunted for a long time, but there was no picture that we could see or feel or catch, with our equipment.

Still I feel more at ease in Los Angeles these days than I used to, having gradually acquired a fair number of friends to look up, check out, and sponge on. I usually stay with Robert Simmons, an old friend who teaches political science at Cal State. Robert lives in Topanga Canyon now, in a thick-walled adobe house with a handsome carved door and a view out and down over the canyon to the hazy rim of the San Fernando Valley. Topanga is just up the coast from Santa Monica: a long, winding, unkempt sort of place, continually threatened by greenness, like a trail hacked through a rain forest. It's hardly a secret wilderness refuge — Topanga Canyon has been well-inhabited since the 1920s, when the movie people discovered it, and the population density is getting pretty dense — and it's not cheap to live here; but it feels hidden even now, with its wild days definitely numbered. The developers have taken most of the other old coast canyons — Malibu, Coldwater. Topanga's turn is next, but not quite yet.

Robert and Audrey Simmons have been living in Topanga Canyon for well over a year, and they still have no more than a glancing relationship with most of their neighbors.

"There's no sense of community here at all," Robert says without regret. "That isn't what people move out to Topanga for. In fact, when I think about it, one of the really significant things about Los Angeles living is the vast number of private worlds that exist side by side without ever touching. Do your thing, stay out of my way, don't lower my real-estate values, and I won't judge you — it's all much more Los Angeles than San Francisco. When there isn't any city, people make their own cities. The instinct is to centralize."

People tell me that quite often in Los Angeles, and it's true that the ones I know best move — or sit quietly — in notably dissimilar cities. Robert Nathan, for instance, lives in Beverly Hills, not far from the Sunset Strip in terms of space, but as distant from it in time as though he and the Strip went around the sun at different paces. His house is cool and still; charged with memories, even to a young stranger, but without the smell of age. The brightness in the house, and the breeze that keeps the age-smell from settling in, is Mrs. Nathan, Helen Shirley, known as Minnie. She is small, and she has red hair; and a nation that is considering the idea of a guaranteed annual income should give serious thought to guaranteeing each man a Minnie Nathan. Some official attempt at Minnie Nathan, anyway.

My friendship with Bob Nathan was close to ten years old before he ever knew about it. I discovered his writing at an age when the normal process was to start becoming Hemingway or Thomas Wolfe. *Portrait of Jenny* and *One More Spring* are the books even people who think he's dead know (and Theodore Bikel's monologue condensation of *The Weans*), but there are others. There have been nearly fifty books, counting the poems and the plays, between *Peter Kindred* in 1919 and *Stonecliff* in 1967.

I've read all of them, give or take a couple. I can't judge them objectively as literature — when a man sits down and reads, not ten, not twenty, but fifty books that another man has written, the fact itself is the judgment of both of them. Robert Nathan's work means something to me as a writer because I learned important things from him — or at least began to learn them, and continue alone now — such things as leanness, and control, and not so much the complete avoidance of self-indulgence as knowing the right time for it. Other writers have learned the same things from Hemingway, or from Chekhov. I learned them from Bob Nathan.

I visit him whenever I'm in Los Angeles. He's seventy-five years old now. His face is tan and lined; sometimes sardonic, more often tired. But the eyes are as quick and attentive as woods eyes still, and the laugh is strong, when it comes. He swims a lot, and still sings (an art he began to study seriously at the age of sixty), and is presently teaching himself to play the cello. On the record rack Lotte Lehmann and the Beatles are side by side.

"I've been working on my autobiography lately. I don't like it. I wish I had something else to be working on, but I don't. There's no fun in this sort of writing — no inventing, and not much discovery. You just sit and remember, and I spend too much time at that without having an excuse for it. But I have to work on something, and that's all there is."

There was a time like this before *Stonecliff*, when all the letters were wearily bitter, describing himself as sitting in the dark waiting to see what would come through the door. Then the new book came, and he got up to meet it one more time. He writes swiftly, once he's started. The letters became joyous and proud while he was working; they seemed to come dancing north like kites. I mention that cycle, but he shakes his head.

"No, I think *Stonecliff* was the last. It was something of an autobiography anyway — getting a novel out of it was a sort of gift, a going-away present. There won't be another one of those."

Fifty years and fifty books. On his desk several old photographs are arranged on a sheet of paper, for possible inclusion in the autobiography. They show him at eighteen and nineteen, sitting in his first car, the kind that had tires like bicycle tires and ran on pure gas, without a carburetor. He and a friend drove down from Cambridge to New York in the spring of 1913, which is as far as he's gotten in the book. It took them three days.

How do you stop being a writer? The years of recognition came during the Depression and lasted through the war. *Portrait of Jennie* was translated into eight languages and made into a movie; so were *One More Spring* and *The Bishop s Wife*. But 1945 is one of those years that defines generations, in literature as in all other worlds. The thing that Robert Nathan had to say, and the manner of his saying, went out of style after the war, as Hemingway's variously begotten children came roaring in. He went on writing: a book a year, or very nearly, and some of them among his best. *The Innocent Eve*, *Sir Henry* (the best of all), *So Love Returns*, *The Mallot Diaries*. You never stop trying to make the thing you make better; or finer, if you can't make it any better. But people think he's dead.

"I suppose I might as well be writing the autobiography," he says in the quiet house. "I don't understand anything that's happening now, not really. I've always disliked hiding in the past, but I can't find any continuity in the world now, or make any sense of it, or say anything about it that would be meaningful, even to myself. And maybe that's a good thing. I don't know."

Over in Hollywood, Jack is still hustling. The Hollywood hustle is pretty much like the Broadway version, at least at a certain level. You wait for other people's decisions, for phone calls that never come. You court backers with ideas for shows; you get involved with phantom productions, where nothing is ever quite signed and no money ever appears; or with great, beached projects where the money is there, but you won't get a credit, and the show is a bomb to begin with, or they wouldn't have been desperate enough to call you in. Most of the time you're dealing with fools and thieves and children, packagers and salesmen, and you generally have to be nice to them. The only thing that can keep you from going mad is to *want*, to be scrambling toward something, for whatever sake. It doesn't always help, of course, and it may even make things worse.

Jack wants to direct movies. He is in his early thirties: a lean, limping, slow-voiced guy with a Mexican jawbone-to-jawbone mustache. He usually works as a dialogue director,

Watts, Los Angeles. Easterners are always surprised at how much greener and more open than Harlem or Dorchester it seems. The tenements of San Francisco and Oakland are more familiar; but in general California is doing away with the traditional suppurating slum neighborhood. The Western version is less messy, and far less visible. The journalist Theodore H. White has written: "Los Angeles is that city in the United States where the Negro probably receives the most decent treatment and has the best opportunities for decent housing."

Al Young told me a story about riding his bike in Palo Alto one evening. His headlight wasn't working, and a cop saw him and yelled, "Hey, boy! Hey, you just get on over here!" From a distance, Al must have looked like some black teen-ager bopping along on his brother's bike; but when the cop got a good look at him, his voice dropped to its tone for Respectable White Adult, and below, into a new category. "Uh, sir — look, I'm sorry I yelled at you, but your light — I mean, did you know your light isn't working? If a car comes along — " The cop was actually shaking. This was just after the riots in East Palo Alto.

224

This is Wiley, a member of the Sons of Watts. We met him by chance, as we wandered into the Sons' headquarters on East 103rd Street just by chance, and he talked with us for a while, and drove over to the Watts Towers with us. All I know about him is in Mike's photograph.

The Sons of Watts came out of the 1965 riot — "the rebellion," as Wiley casually but invariably puts it. "We were all on the streets that night. I don't know anybody who didn't throw a rock, maybe pick himself up a radio or a suit of clothes. I can't say anybody's ashamed of it, either." Most of them were unemployed high school dropouts, and many had police records; though, as Wiley says, all that's necessary to have a record in Watts — and therefore be unemployed — is to be black. On the surface, an unlikely group to begin beautifying the ghetto, and fostering civic pride.

Yet this is exactly what has happened in Watts since the night of the rebellion. Today the Sons of Watts sweep the streets, clean yards, paint houses and fix furniture; sponsor dances, picnics, and outings; stand guard at dangerous crosswalks; paint and distribute trash cans, and empty the cans when they're filled. They were the moving force behind the successful 1967 Watts Summer Festival; and in that same year they held a retreat with members of the police force, with the aim of opening communications between those who live in Watts and those who occupy it. They also work at finding jobs for blacks, at bringing industry into the district to create jobs, and at developing self-sustaining cooperatives within Watts. One of their minor projects — all but unique in the new black movement — is to combat anti-Semitism within the ghetto.

As they have done since they came into existence, the Sons of Watts patrol the streets regularly, turning up quietly at places where trouble may happen, and usually managing either to forestall or control it. "We're better than the cops," Wiley says, "because we aren't cops. They cause more trouble than they stop — come in yelling and waving their guns and beating heads right and left. Nobody calls the cops for anything. But people call us when they need help. They think we're beautiful."

But Watts remains what it was four years ago, for all the official surveys; and for all the efforts to make life prouder and a little more bearable. "People don't live in Watts because they want to," Wiley says. "Not yet." He thinks that Watts could easily explode again, given the right moment's mixture of rage and hopelessness. "Every damn thing that caused the rebellion, it's still right here. Some people have changed, but this place hasn't. And nobody really thinks the white man will act right unless he's scared not to. I'll tell you one thing that's different, though. Next time, I don't think they'd mess up Watts. That's changed, anyway."

which is a curious, without-portfolio sort of profession that may cover anything from coaching actors to rewriting the script, to finding coffee in moments of crisis. There is no union of dialogue directors. Most of them are trying to break into some other union.

These days Jack is writing scripts for a TV travelogue series; but he still maintains his own small production company, and he still looks out for stories and properties and options. He only took on this present gig because there was a possibility that from that point he might get to direct a series of his own. It seems less likely now, for a variety of reasons; but essentially because that is the nature of the hustle.

He takes me over to a lot at the Goldwyn Studios where they're shooting a Western with Gregory Peck and Eva Marie Saint. It's a huge, dim, chilly place: there are catwalks and flats, and ropes hanging out of the darkness, the way it is backstage in a theatre; but there are a couple of trailers too, and a full-sized log cabin with oneside out. The studio is swarming with people. One man sits off alone at a big console, monitoring the sound; middle-aged men drag electric cables, move lights, wash the windows of the cabin. Behind us is a backdrop of a pine forest, painted on canvas, and there are a lot of real pine branches lying around too, on real dirt. There are hills, folded into a grandstand shape, gray and maroon in the shadows. They feel as light as toys when you touch them, and Jack says they photograph like toys.

"This is death," he says, nodding at the double row of chairs that face the cutaway end of the log cabin. Some of the people who are watching Peck and Miss Saint rehearse a scene are obviously part of the movie, but not all of them. The director orders furniture moved, decides to do without a couple of plates on the table, tries having Eva Marie Saint cross at a slightly different angle and use her left arm for a gesture instead of her right; and the onlookers fold their arms and murmur sideways. It's a little like a trial scene. "This is death," Jack says. "I couldn't work like this. I mean, I could work, but I couldn't direct. I like to shoot in the streets."

He is uncomfortable, and a bit sad, and it shows. "I always feel like that when I'm on a lot. I never feel as though I belong, except as a director. I've been making my living in this business since 1955, but I've never really been of it — just on the fringes. You could start in Hollywood today and be about as far along as I am."

Gregory Peck looks exactly like Gregory Peck in the movies — unbelievably, monstrously so. There should be some sort of distance between Peck listening in the cabin to Eva Marie Saint as she tells him about her Plains childhood, and Peck listening to the director correcting his handling of a line, but there isn't one. It's hard to explain. He looks too real, too familiar, like a great actor's caricature of Gregory Peck. The lines add to this feeling: the stylized strophes and antistrophes of the classic Western. "You get to a lot of places, don't you?" she says to him, and he answers, "I don't stop."

Jack is watching the grips and gaffers and soundmen moving around with the enviable sureness of people who have a salable skill and a good union. "There's a world," he says quietly. "There's a great family feeling that grows up between these guys, working on the same set. They may not see each other for years after that, but they remember. I recognize a lot of the faces — I've worked with them — but I don't know if they'd remember me."

I had dinner with the Lumsdens and the Weavers last night. Marshall Lumsden is the editor of *West*, the Sunday magazine of the Los Angeles *Times*, and John Weaver is a freelance writer and lecturer. Between the two of them, they know as much about Los Angeles as any decent man would want to know. The Lumsdens live in Santa Monica; John and Harriett Weaver live in Beverly Hills.

Barbara Lumsden is a New Yorker, and she would love to go home. Los Angeles is great for theatre, but the presence of the beach is a handicap when you're trying to get your children educated. (This is a real occupational hazard of living in Southern and Central California. In New York, in the winter, school is about the only place to go where it's warm and you don't have to spend any money.) But Marshall, who is from Indiana, and has divided his time between both coasts since the war, votes thoughtfully for Los Angeles. "It's the weather, I suppose," he says, "and then somehow I'm much more curious about Los Angeles than I am about New York. It may just be the pace, and that incredible rate of obsolescence, but I always feel as though everything's happening here. Maybe nothing is. There's so much energy around; so much raw, pure ambition. It's the only place I've ever lived where one of the main rackets is thinking up brand-new rackets for other people to go into. It's a film place, it just keeps unreeling."

John Weaver, whom I would have expected to like San Francisco, cordially detests it. "San Francisco is a damp, dull, rude, dirty city, a hick town giving itself unbearable airs over culture it hasn't got. And they know it. San Franciscans used to be the most arrogant people in the world, but they're becoming very defensive now. Berkeley's fine, though. Berkeley's still a darling."

The question of whether it's easier to be poor in Los Angeles or New York came up, and Marshall suggested that it might be a worse scene out west. "It never looks as bad, the way Watts doesn't look anything like Harlem, but there's a coldness. California isn't very generous to failures. You're supposed to make it here — this is the second-chance state, after all — and if you can't invent some sort of success for yourself, there's just no use wasting time on you. Reagan speaks for that coldness, but you can feel it all the way down the line."

But Harriett Weaver, who can take care of herself under any circumstances and still look nice, answered, "I've been poor here, and I've been poor in New York, and there's no comparison. Cold hearts I can cope with, but not New York, not in the winter. It's the hopelessness as much as the cold — they go together. Here at least you can sleep on the beach, and there really is fresh fruit just for the picking. People write about the Dust Bowl migrants finding out that it wasn't true about the oranges, but it's still true even now. I know exactly where I'd start copping food and fruit, if we had to."

Random Los Angeles thoughts, mostly thought while driving the freeways. The only thing of any significance that I can say about the freeways is that I'm always being astonished at the quickness and ease with which the human can get used to anything. There's money in the freeways, surely — there's money to be made off docile captives. Look at the street entertainers who work the patient queues of London: a cottage craft, of course, compared to the things American knowhow will do, once somebody fully conceives of the inexhaustible market — parched, weary, angry, bored — waiting down there for the wreckage to be hauled away. It would start with helicopters, I suppose.

If you're on the freeway by 3:30 P.M., there's an excellent chance that you'll get home for supper. This fact sets the Los Angeles rhythm, as the two-hour *siesta* makes the pace in other countries. The rush hour has gotten a good deal earlier everywhere since I was a boy.

Some days you can see the mountains, some days you can't. They are brown and gaunt and small, but their suddenness, after a week's absence, is what makes them invariably impressive. You forget very easily that Los Angeles has mountains, just as you tend to forget that it's on the sea, in spite of the coast road. There isn't a truly level sidewalk anywhere in San Francisco, but Los Angeles is essentially flat. There are hills, but they're going as wantonly as the bison, and they'd be harder to preserve because they don't mate. Between the flatness and the air, Los Angeles often feels like part of the San Joaquin Valley.

The Los Angeles coast is beautiful, but it's vanishing too, into private hands. From the Will Rogers State Park north through Malibu, as far as Carillo Beach, it's all clubs and cottages; mostly fancy-cheap, which is the worst kind, especially near the sea.

Ironically, both the sea and the mountains contribute to the smog problem here. Jack explained it to me. The ozone, which is sort of the active ingredient of smog — the master of ceremonies, as it were — comes off the water; and the smog itself piles up against the mountains and stays there until a wind clears it away. Paris gets that way in the winter, when the sky is heavy and none of the normal effusions and exudations of the city can get out. Mike and I were in downtown Los Angeles one afternoon when the rain came down black, hurting our eyes.

At night in Topanga, the Santa Ana wind comes booming around the house, though the days are very still. It's early this year, according to Robert — you don't usually start getting the Santa Ana until August, like the mistral. August is a bad month to have a steady wind blowing in Southern California. Topanga hasn't had a real fire since Robert and Audrey have been here, but the possibility is present all the time. It's another one of those things you get used to living with.

There's a big news kiosk on Fairfax Avenue that sells pornographic books: not merely poor, prim *Fanny Hill* and the windy Marquis, but really dirty stuff, humorless and ungrammatical; classical smut, as opposed to the literate frivolities of the Olympia Press. The funny part is that at this corner Fairfax is a middle-class Jewish neighborhood, very much like the block where I grew up. Delicatessens, butcher shops, bakeries, modest residential apartments, the works. The nice ladies meet on the corner and chat about their grown daughters or the nephew in college, serenely ignoring both the children who pick at them and the flushing, furtive men breathing raggedly over *The Ordeal of the Rod* and *Linda's Strange Vacation*. *Hamishe* is the word.

Chandler invented Los Angeles for me — I'm coming to realize that more and more, as I'm here. The Los Angeles of *The High Window* has been gone for a long time, though bits of it still cling on in the bends of the freeways. It's the rhythm of things that has changed, even more than the physical scene. But it's still Philip Marlowe's world that I glimpse and smell and sense, wandering around: room clerks, houseboys; tired, pretty women and tired, ugly cops, and old elevator men in decaying hotels, sleeping on stools with their mouths open; heat and age and sudden rain; big, cool houses in Pasadena and Bel-Air, and the places that are more than big — "great silent estates, with twelve-foot walls and wrought-iron gates and ornamental hedges; and inside, if you could get inside, a special brand of sunshine, very quiet, put up in noise-proof containers just for the upper classes." Palms, deodars, acacias; orange groves and lemon groves; sage, scrub oak, and manzanita in the foothills. Danger, and some gallantry; and seediness, always.

You don't read Chandler for the style he was so proud of, or for character — except Marlowe's — or for plot. (Even the staunchest Chandler fans can't tell you what happens in any of the books; it's a very good way to win small bets.) You read him for the eye: not the full glance, but the peripheral vision, the things seen far off to the side. Everything in Chandler's writing dates and dissolves and parodies itself, except for that strange understanding of the truths that don't date, the Los Angeles that does not change. He may be the only man who knew it, the continuing Los Angeles.

> *It was getting dark outside now. The rushing sound of the traffic had died a little, and the air from the open window, not yet cool from the night, had that tired end-of-the-day smell of dust, automobile exhaust, sunlight rising from hot walls and sidewalks, the remote smell of food in a thousand restaurants, and perhaps, drifting down from the residential hills above Hollywood — if you had a nose like a hunting dog — a touch of that peculiar tomcat smell that eucalyptus trees give off in warm weather.*

He wasn't a very good poet, but he's the only one Los Angeles has ever had.

Today Robert has to speak at the graduation ceremony of the Orange County Peace Officers' Academy — my friend Robert, with his bushy grenadier mustache, and his signature on all those full-page ads in the Sunday *Times*! It seems that Captain Derald Hunt, who's in charge of the graduation, took a political science seminar from Robert last year, and was, if not altogether converted to flower power, seriously shook up, which is almost the same thing for a policeman. He's become concerned that his young cops are being taught to function in a world that no longer exists; and that sending them into the streets of Los Angeles is a lot like ordering Swiss Guards to Vietnam. So Robert is going to speak on "The Changing Role of Modern Day Law Enforcement," and I'm to wait at the curb with the motor running.

We've been making nervous little jokes like that all week. Los Angeles cops, to begin with — and in Orange County! Orange County — oh boy, in my small circle of friends that is *it*, that's the Bad Place: the selfish, frightened, secret heart of America. Goldwater country., George Wallace country, the country of the rotting dream — the place where they think Lyndon Johnson's a Communist, but know exactly what he meant about three billion of Them and two hundred million of Us. Enemy territory. I've never been here before today, but it's part of my emotional geography. *Here there be tygers.* They must feel that way about Berkeley.

The graduation is being held at the Theo Lacy Security Facility — a prison referred to by policemen as "the country club." Forty-five officers, representing eleven police departments, are taking part in the ceremony. Their parents are here; their kid brothers and their girls, and, in many cases, their children. The whole scene is the epitome of squareness, of a white-picket-fence, hunting-with-Dad world that I've never known, except as an image. I rather envied it when I was a boy in the Bronx, and I mock it bitterly now, but it's still an image. Who would marry a cop, who would father one? I don't know anything about these people.

There is to be a review. The cops line up at the far end of the parking lot and come marching down behind a color guard. It's a sloppy parade, irresistibly and wistfully reminiscent of graduations from the sixth grade. But the fathers take pictures, and the wives hold their babies as high as their bouffants, saying, "Look, look, there's Daddy!" A lot of dogs are barking, making a strained, frantic sound. The jail is just across from the county pound.

After the visiting police chiefs review the graduates, they march off again, and then break ranks and come to find their families. They are very young, most of them, even the ones who have children. It's easy to imagine them getting dressed for the ceremony, shining their shoes, buttoning their summer uniform shirts, tying their black ties over and over. Now, released and relaxed, the faces are pretty good — not terribly bright or serious, but not stupid either, and not mean. High school faces, beach faces, none of them long past acne. Well, which faces beat up the housewives and children and pregnant women on the night of June 21, 1967, in Los Angeles? Somebody did.

If you turn your head, you can see the prisoners: five or six men in gray denim, behind the wire fence, sitting in the grass. I can't read their faces from here, but it sure does tighten things up another notch. I try to imagine them putting on their clothes and brushing their teeth, but that's harder.

The lunch is regular jail fare, according to Derald Hunt, and it's certainly no worse than the stuff I ate for four years in college. The cooks are prisoners too; their faces, as

Pershing Square

they ladle out the roast beef, mashed potatoes, and canned succotash, are as young as the young officers' faces, but more immediate, more shocking in their humanness. They smile politely at me, and I smile dreadfully at them.

I like Derald Hunt, cop or no cop. There's a vulnerable quality about him, a lack of the protective numbness that these young ones will almost surely have to make around themselves. Derald is dark, with a face that is always a little worried. Mid-forties, probably; old enough to have broken into police work the old way. "They gave me a badge and a stick, took me to a wall map and traced out what looked like half the city, told me that was my beat, and sent me off alone in a car. Later on, when they could spare a man, they paired me off with an old-timer. I worked with him for three months, and that was all the training I ever had."

They don't do that any more, by the way, send rookies and veterans out together. "We avoid teams as much as we can," Derald says, "because the fact is that two cops will get into trouble where a single man won't. There's a tendency to show off for each other,

California youth

especially when you have a young cop showing an older guy that he's not chicken. Courage, proving your courage, is very important to policemen.''

There is only one black officer in the group. Derald isn't sure whether he's the second or the third Negro to graduate from the Orange County Peace Officers' Academy, out of thirty-seven classes. "I know it's bad," he says. "I know damn well that it's hard for Negroes to get on just about any police force you want to name. But there's another side to it, which is that fewer and fewer Negroes are trying to get into police work these days. It's understandable — I suppose they undergo a certain amount of ostracism in their own communities — but of course, it's a vicious circle. Communication gets pretty feeble, I know it.''

Talking about the young cops, and about the reason he wanted Robert to come and speak to them, he leans forward and his voice takes on an edge of urgency. "The policeman today doesn't know what the hell people want of him. He's in a much tougher position than the policeman of twenty years ago, because the public attitude toward him is much more fragmented and confused than it was then. He doesn't know what he's supposed to be any more, or even who he's responsible to. The new legal reforms bewilder him — frankly, it's a hard thing for him, when he's out there on the street, to be exactly as concerned for the rights of a criminal, protect them just as earnestly as he does your rights and mine. I'm not saying the reforms are bad, or unnecessary. I'm just saying that policemen work hard, and they're underpaid and vastly undertrained for people who are asked to be watchmen, psychologists, sociologists, youth workers, historians, and politicians. Seven weeks at a school like this doesn't begin to make a dent in the things they have to know and understand. That's why I thought Dr. Simmons might be able to tell them a few things they're not likely to hear from other cops. It may be the last chance they'll have to listen.''

He is silent for a while, and then goes on, "It's the sensitive ones who really have the rough time. The insensitive officers, the ones who are just concerned with what they can get away with and what they can't, they catch on to changes that concern them pretty quickly. But the others, they really want to be liked, they really would like to do the right thing, and they're the ones who wind up feeling they're damned whatever they do. And they're the ones who get into the worst trouble sometimes.''

A couple of times during the meal, graduating officers come up to Derald to complain about their class standing. They are very specific about it: I outscored this guy here, and here and here, so how come he's ranked higher than I am? The competition is pretty bitter, according to Derald; not only among individuals, but between the different services. The notebooks of the best students are exhibited on a table outside, for visitors to inspect.

Looking over the notebooks, you literally don't know whether to laugh or cry. They are amazingly thick and thorough for seven weeks' study: neatly divided into sections covering traffic violations, sex crimes, narcotics, race relations, fingerprinting, homicide, car theft — even a chapter on the art of writing lucid reports. But the great mass of the stuff is simply printed lecture material, supplemented by the student's own notes in the margin, and the notes themselves are depressingly identical. The section on race relations, for instance, is admirable for a police notebook. It says that Negroes are human beings, and emphasizes that they have the same desire to better themselves that everybody else has. So all the officers duly write it down "*Negroes human beings.*" It's parroting, almost all of it, transcribing, the way they did in high school. There's an echoing absence of personality in the notes, which makes the occasional misspellings rather endearing. You have to take your personal touches where you can get them, and be grateful.

Well, maybe it's better like this. When they do start thinking on their own, they can be scary in a different way. One of the class leaders has deduced from the lectures that "*black militants the enemy, not bulk of black people.*" Any adjustment is possible, just so you still have an enemy. And there's another guy who hasn't quite understood the really restrained, liberal part about Communists and ghetto riots. Or maybe he's understood it very well, and I haven't.

Robert makes his speech in the prison auditorium, speaking from a podium that has him throwing his words a long way down to the folding chairs. He doesn't like it, but maybe that's what they're used to. It's a good speech, at any altitude. He begins bravely by quoting Heraclitus's statement that society is in a constant process of becoming, and goes on to talk about the meaning of blue and olive uniforms in this time.

> *The joy, excitement, and benefits of learning give way to strident discontent and disorder. The affluent society spawns hippie dropouts. The black man's aspiration to affluence yields to resentment, frustration, and racial unrest. A free society using compulsory military service produces resistance to such compulsion. The use of free assembly merges into civil disobedience. . . .*
>
> *Amidst these broad symptoms of a society undergoing profound change, you, the policeman, must contend with the daily tasks of traffic control, crimes to person and property, and civil disorder . . . This is the hard spot, to maintain the status quo while deep social change occurs. . . .*

The dogs have never stopped barking. Just behind me, three small children are playing on the floor. A baby is crying; a woman fixes her hair by feel; a father is trying to change the film in his camera. The two cops sitting to my left and right are older than most of the others. There are several like that here, for a refresher course, or just to see the graduation. Without exception, they have the *thickness* that I've always associated with policemen — thickness of neck, of hands, of features, thickness of surface and sympathy. Walking walls. The young ones don't look like that at all, whatever they write in their notebooks.

> *We are each of us human. We are each of us a citizen. My link to you is our shared humanity.*

Robert, I don't believe it. The kids, yes, but not these. But if I don't believe they're human, what must the people of Watts think they are? Will all the young cops look — feel — like that in a few years; is the thickening already at work on them? Robert tells that bad story about the fireman he met who couldn't wait for the summer riots to break out — he wanted to get himself a couple of niggers. What do they think about *that*, these parents, these girl friends? How are they on shared humanity? *Policemen human beings.* I need to write that down somewhere.

> *I believe in supporting my local police. Each of you are vital to my well being, my family's well being, and my community's well being. We must continue to talk together, no matter how noisy and threatening the din around us becomes — our mutual survival depends upon it. Protection of the status quo is no longer your challenge; rather, it is to understand the changes we are undergoing, and to change with those changes by identifying and supporting those values that are essential to the maintenance of the dignity of each of us.*

Do they hear him? There are the dogs all the time, and jets coming over, and that damn Mount Sinai podium, and the children are restless. "*We have all done things we should not have done.*" They applaud, and a few mothers come up to Robert afterward; but the only comment I hear from any of the men is one young officer saying to another, "Boy, I'd sure hate to have to take lecture notes from that guy!" Derald liked it, anyway. Derald really admires Robert.

We stay for a while after the graduation (they walked across the stage to get their diplomas with nice, silly, red-faced grins), waiting for one of the jail people to take us around the place. Derald comes along, never having been through Theo Lacy himself. Our guide is a clerk: jowly, middle-aged, jovial. He has a peculiar transparency for a fat man, as though he had once been full of pale orange syrup, like those oldtime wax kazoos and false teeth. They used to turn that color when the syrup was all sucked out.

Theo Lacy is a minimum-security prison. The men don't live in cells, but in large barracks, and they stroll freely on the neat grass without any obvious jail rhythm on them. Most are serving time for misdemeanors — drunkenness, drunken driving, some for desertion; a few sex offenders. They have that work-furlough program here, where an inmate can find a job on the outside, drive his own car to work every day, wearing civilian clothes, and return to the prison at night. There are "week-enders," too: men who spend every Saturday and Sunday in jail, working out their sentences two days at a time. The country club. It's not a hard place to escape from, if you want to. "Just step over the fence, that's all," the fat clerk says. "The rate always starts going up about this time of year. Nice weather, the boys start getting a bit restless. They can't ever come back here, though, if they escape, not here."

He shows us through the central building, where banks of switches and circuits control doors, windows, lights, temperature, alarm systems — everything in this placid jail that needs to be controlled. Derald is particularly interested — he likes gadgets. He's a nut on helicopters, and wishes all police departments had them. There were helicopters hanging over the crowd on the night of June 21, with guns in the doors.

"And here's the hotbox," the fat man says. "Where we keep the bad boys."

It's a big door, wood and steel, exactly like the door to a meat locker. Someone is singing far away behind it — not really singing; a long, deep drone without words, going up and going down. The fat man hauls the door open, and the sound stops.

"Yessir," the voice says. "How you all doing out there?" The daylight behind us glints off the bars. Six doors, but only one face: white and amused, lightning. "How's it going out there?" Can he see us looking at him, or would he be dazzled? *Can he see us?* We step back together, and the clerk closes the door. The singing begins again.

"What are people put in there for?" Robert asks. "Fighting, things like that?"

The fat man leans back on his heels and wrenches his knuckles. "No-o-o, there's not much fighting goes on here. It's mostly, oh, refusing to work, not obeying the rules, being where they're not supposed to be. Like a lot of them will sneak over to another barracks, try to scrounge a few cigarettes. Well, that's the hotbox right there." He smiles. "Course, you can't really call it a hotbox — it's actually pretty cold and miserable. It's supposed to be."

Derald asks in a very low voice, "How long will he be in? How long do they stay, a few hours? A day?

"More like three, four days," the fat man says. "That's about the average. It depends. We had this hippie in a while ago, he spent his whole sentence behind that door. Said he wasn't going to work, wasn't going to do anything. He was in there forty-five days. His whole sentence."

"Well, but you keep track, don't you? I mean, you know who's locked up there, and how long he's supposed to stay. There wouldn't be any chance of somebody just being forgotten." Derald is speaking very quickly, much faster than usual. "You keep records."

The fat man smiles at us again. He's got us now, the professor and the beatnik, and most especially the fancy cop. He's got us exactly the way that face in the cell had us, and his smile is the same. Did you get to thinking it wasn't really prison, after all? Did you think it was all right? "Oh, we keep records."

"That's good," Derald says. He manages to laugh. "Wow, I'd sure hate to be locked up in that place and just forgotten."

"Well, sure," the clerk says. "Who wouldn't?"

Venice, white, rotting Venice. I don't really like this place — I smell death, and it frightens me — but I always seem to wind up walking around here. It's one of the very few places in Los Angeles where you can walk along and sometimes see something happen on the street. Nobody ever writes that Los Angeles is a strangely quiet city. Even the downtown area, which feels a little like downtown New York, with its grimy warehouses and office buildings, the secondhand shoe stores, the Farmers' Market, the drugstores with trusses in the windows, the smell of Mexican cooking, and the charging, indifferent crowds churning up the curiously comforting mess that people make — even this is utterly deserted after six or seven o'clock; as still as night Merced or Weaverville, and far emptier. In Latin cities, people live in the streets; in that sense, Los Angeles is the most American city of all. We have always tended to be a much more private, secretive people than anyone's mythology gives us credit for being.

But Venice is a little different. It has an odd history: it was laid out in 1904 as an American replica of the real Venice: canals, gondolas, Renaissance buildings and bridges, and everything. (Disney didn't invent it, nor did Hearst; this passion for working models of other worlds.) The original enterprise was sickly from the beginning, and died in the 1920's; but during the Depression Venice was reborn as Coney Island, and it did very well for some time. Chandler's Los Angeles came here to play.

You couldn't tell it now. There's nothing left of either incarnation, except the canals, the odd little stone groves along the beach front, and a lot of old cottages and empty store windows. It's a city of old people, more like Far Rockaway than Coney — by day,

Venice junk shop

237

anyway. But at night the kids come out of hiding (it feels like that), and then Venice becomes a little like that other one: warrened, alleyed, full of quick footsteps and muffled laughter; the most mysterious of all cities, and the most desperate.

On the other side of the street, a tall woman stalks swiftly out of a house, towing a little girl along with her. She isn't a pretty woman; she seems to be marching straight toward middle age with no particularly happy memories, but with some toughness. Everything moves slowly in daytime Venice: I forget about her for what seems like a long time, and then look back to see that she's still hurrying, far away across the street. A man comes around the corner and stands in her way. He looks somewhat younger than she, and he's drunk. She tries to duck around him, never letting go of the child, but he won't let her by.

It's impossible to hear what they're saying to each other. Someone is playing an electric guitar in one of the blank white buildings, and there's traffic passing between. In his drunkenness, the man moves as weightlessly as a dancer, stroking her, weaving his arms around her, while she first pushes at him and then stands very still, being heavy for both of them. The little girl looks calmly away into the street, and the guitar chimes and whines.

At last, the tall woman sags slightly at the knees and holds the man with her free arm: limp, drowned. He hugs her, talking close into her ear, but suddenly she breaks free of him and starts across the street. He yells silently; he goes partway after her; but she means it this time. The grace leaves him. He watches her go for a little, shouts a sound, and then lunges off down the street, aiming himself into the door that she came out of.

A block farther on, there's a hippie store: the usual baubles-bangles-and-beads place inside, but with a window almost identical with the dead storefronts on either side. The Los Angeles Police Department obviously has the same policy toward hippies that the Chinese have about marauding birds — never let them land, never let them roost, give them no rest, until they fall. The San Francisco Underground is practically a part of the city Establishment, but Los Angeles resists the debasement of language. Here, underground still means underground.

Always read the bulletin board in a hippie joint, however long it takes. You never know. Among the ads for Triumphs, drivers, and rhythm guitarists, and the ones that say *Susan, we love you, call collect, Mom and Dad*, I come across this notice:

> ARE YOU TIRED OF CALIFORNIA, REAGAN, AND THE
> MAN? MOVE TO YOUNGSTOWN, OHIO. IT'S CLEAN.
> A NEW HOME FOR GOOD PEOPLE. CONTACT JIM BAKER,
> 427 SHERMAN CANAL, VENICE.

People from All Over

Artists in San Francisco

Santa Barbara school

Hippies in Golden Gate Park

Girl looking for gold in Sacramento River

George Barris Kustom City in North Hollywood. Barris has only one or two rivals
for pre-eminence as a designer of custom automobiles, and none to dispute his claim of having
made the field both respectable and commercially profitable. In the world of floating grilles,
fadeaway fenders, naugahyde tops, and caterpillar-type exhaust headers — best drawn by Tom
Wolfe in The Kandy-Kolored Tangerine-Flake Streamline Baby—George Barris
is the artist-king. He designs vehicles to the gadgety specifications of movies and TV shows
(the proliferating kind in which, as he says, "the car is the real hero"); as well as for
the personal use of many public people, mostly actors. In addition, he produces car shows, acts as
an advisor for the Ford Custom Car Caravan, and oversees an extensive line of accessories
and scale models based on his creations. They sell like mad.

Tom Wolfe thinks that car styling is one of the true folk arts of twentieth-century
America, and that the work of George Barris, "Big Daddy" Roth, and others represents the last
stage before the museums and scholars get hold of it. I think he's right; what's more argu-
able is his reiterated belief in Barris as an American Brancusi. Barris seems more the fine,
intelligent, loving craftsman, taking conventional lines as logically far as they will
go. Granted, you can only do so much with Liberace's taste in Cadillacs, or Elvis Presley's
in Rolls-Royces; with the Batmobile, the Munster Koach, the Drag-u-la, or Sonny
and Cher's matched Mustangs. (My sneaky favorite is the car with the door that opens down-
ward, made expressly to reveal a specified amount of leg when Mamie van Doren or
somebody gets into it.)

Barris himself is a very nice man, happily doing exactly what he wants to do; though
he admits that the rush of commercial jobs is leaving him less time than he likes to work on his
own ideas. Yet he still seems proud and excited at the thought of customizing a car for
someone like Bobby Darin or Barry Goldwater. He likes to mention the fact that his wife has
designed some of the more luxurious interiors, and that Tom Wolfe praised her
paintings when he was at the house. He is concerned with honesty. He dreams of working
with Maserati.

These students are members of Jerry Friedberg's history seminar at U.C. Davis. On the day that Mike and I visited them, they were discussing the social origins of the American Revolution; not as teacher and taperecorders, but as equal contributors, and as close friends. I liked it a lot better than the way I studied history.

At the end of the class, one of the students, who had been absent for a couple of weeks, said wistfully, "I felt sort of an outsider today. Lonesome."

"I'm sorry," Jerry said and there was a hesitant but almost visible moving toward the young man on the part of the others. Jerry looked around at them and said, "Let's grock, okay?"

Grocking is a concept out of Robert A. Heinlein's novel Stranger in a Strange a Land, a true "underground" book, which has caught on amazingly among a wide variety of people; mostly for its ideas of community and Communication. To grock, roughly, is to dig a person or a thing, only more so.

They stood up then, in a circle, and piled their hands together, like that game you play with children. It seemed a little awkward and formal — because of our presence, I think — but it was lovely too, and somehow valiant. Afterward, most of them hugged the one who felt lonesome.

It's an Esalen Institute technique, of course; recalling to my narrow mind all those sad, successful losers who want to sign up for dancing lessons from Zorba the Greek. Yet I do like the things Jerry is trying with his classes — the walks, the weekend retreats together, the idea of grading oneself, the grocking business, the sessions in which everything but the American Revolution may be discussed; the attempt to involve students and teacher with each other in more than one dimension, for more than a couple of hours every week. There's a grave silliness about it all, but I think it's very important.

Because the other alternative is the way I went to college, which really hasn't changed much in the last ten years, for all the noise and all the new gadgets. On the undergraduate level, at least, it's still mostly a matter of serving your time and getting your piece of paper. California, which has produced both the awesome, unstoppable "multiversity" and the wild revolt against it — whose echoes have only begun to be heard — is starting now to break out with independent educational ventures: some within the system, like Jerry's classes, and some parallel to it, like the Free Universities. Somewhere in the confusion, the real future is stirring. Incidentally, Jerry Friedberg has been fired by U. C. Davis, presumably for the experimental aspects of his classes. He thinks that's what it must be, anyway — Davis has never given a reason.

LIST OF COLOR PHOTOGRAPHS

Following page 32

BARON WOLMAN. *Marina, Los Angeles*

J. R. EYERMAN. *Los Angeles*

NEIL LAKATA. *Downtown Los Angeles*

NEIL LAKATA. *Golden State and Pasadena Freeway Interchange*

ANSEL ADAMS. *Livermore Valley*

FRED LYON. *Sea Ranch, Northernmost Sonoma Coast*

MICHAEL BRY. *Panamint Mountains*

ANSEL ADAMS. *Lone Pine Peak, Sierra Nevada*

ANSEL ADAMS. *Joshua Tree National Monument*

Following page 192

PHILIP HYDE. *Ano Nuevo Island, Santa Cruz County Coast*

MICHAEL BRY. *Bode, Mono County*

MICHAEL BRY. *Mendocino*

MICHAEL BRY. *Tinsley Island, Sacramento River delta country*

PHILIP HYDE. *Jedadiah Smith Redwood Park, Del Norte County*

MICHAEL BRY. *Pebble Beach*

JOHN WAGGAMAN. *Salk Institute for Biological Studies, La Jolla*

MICHAEL BRY. *Yosemite Falls*

MICHAEL BRY. *View from Sentinel Dome, Yosemite Park*

LIST OF BLACK AND WHITE PHOTOGRAPHS